© **December 2019 – All Rights Reserved.**

ISBN: 9781980592174

Disclaimers
Nothing in this book should be construed as legal advice, tax advice, medical advice, or psychological advice. Seek qualified, professional help as appropriate for your unique situation.

While everything in this book has been thoroughly researched and is presented as accurate as of the publication date (December 2019), things can change at any time. Use your brain, do your own research, and keep your ear to the ground for changes.

One more thing: Any monetary amounts quoted in this book are in US dollars unless otherwise specified.

Table of Contents

Acknowledgements 9
Foreword by Sharon Gourlay 11
Notes from writing the 3rd edition 15
Intro 17
    What is a digital nomad? 23
    What digital nomads *are* 28
    What digital nomads are *not* 31
    Questions you've had about digital nomads 33
    but were afraid to ask 33
    How to use this book 36
    Experience and perspective — about the author and contributors 37
    Is this the right time to become a nomad? 39
    Eight steps to becoming a digital nomad (and an interim section) 41
Step 1: know yourself and what you want **43**
    Worksheet #1: know yourself 45
    Some important things to start working on: passports and visas 47
    Worksheet #2: what's important to you? 50
    Some possible destinations 51
    Worksheet #3: brainstorming 56
    Resources for researching your potential destinations ... 57
    Find your 'why' 59
    Know the political climate 59
    Worksheet #4: the finalists — my most likely destinations 61
    Wrapping it all up 62
Step 2: Clarify your desires and acknowledge limitations **63**
    Worksheet #5: Clarifying desires 64
    Nomads vs. expats 65

Getting ready — what to do next 66
Finding a new place to live 66
Living with a host family 67
Co-living space 68
Get your own place 69
Find the perfect place 71
House-sitting 73
RV's — a home on wheels 75
Other options 77
Home vs. Base 78
Ways to deal with your stuff 78
Cleaning house — throw it away 80
Make some money for your journey: sell it 81
Be generous — give it away 81
The option of last resort — store it 82
Take it with you 82
Nostalgia and memories 83
The minimalist philosophy — and its rewards 84
Budgeting: the 64,000,000-yen question 85
Worksheet #6: monthly expenses 86
Other possible limitations to consider 89
Soft skills — strengths, not limitations 91
Other considerations 93
Who's coming with you? Traveling with others 93
Traveling with partner / spouse 94
Traveling with children 97
Traveling for the LGBT community 99
Worksheet #7: The plan 101

Nomadus interruptus: just a test, please 103
The five questions of the Nomadus Interruptus test 104

Worksheet #8: Putting it all together for a test 107
During the test… 109
Now that the test is over 109
Worksheet #9: post-test: how's it going? 110
   Do any of these statements fit how you felt? 112
What if it's not for me? 113

Step 3: Making money as a nomad 115

A quick word on flag theory 116
Working with your existing job 118
Working on your own 119
Co-working spaces 121
So, what *do* you do to make money? 123
The list of opportunities 125
Sales and marketing 125
Teaching jobs 126
I'm a people person! 128
Technical jobs 129
Artsy jobs for the creative types 131
Pound-the-keyboard jobs 135
Money and legal jobs 138
Help people travel better 139
Offline service jobs 140
Worksheet #10: What do you want to do to make money?
.... 143
Where to find jobs 145
Volunteering 148
Should I incorporate my business? 151
Tax stuff 155
   Basics for Americans 157
   Basics for Canadians 157

    Basics for Europeans 158
    Basics for Australians 159
    Basics for New Zealanders 159
What if I'm not a resident *anywhere*? 160
Moving and accessing money 160
Start with a bank account 161
Add a Paypal account 163
Consider a credit card 165
Other options for Americans 166
Other options for Europeans 167
Other options for almost everyone 168
Cryptocurrencies 169
Wrapping it all up 172

Step 4: get affairs in order 173
Your anchor 174
All about that (home)base 175
Some other loose ends to tie up before leaving 176
    Let's not forget about our health before leaving. 178
    Let's talk about sex, just for a second. 180
Stay connected by voice 181
Paperwork 183
In-case-of-emergency letters 183
Wills 184
Learning the local language 185
Travel insurance 185
Medical tourism 190
Book your travel 191
Wrapping it all up 194

Step 5: Gear up and slim down 195
Personal item 197

Laptop bag	197
Backpacks	198
Carry-on / checked luggage	199
What to pack	201
What *not* to pack	204
What you might want to pack	205
Wrapping it all up	205
Step 6: The Big Move and settling in	**206**
The final countdown	206
Leaving	208
You are a tourist	211
Arriving	212
Wrapping things up	216
Step 7: Start enjoying your new life	**217**
Worksheet #11: Now that you're settled in...	218
As stuff goes...	220
Speaking of stuff — what about shopping?	222
Avoiding censorship	223
Creating routine	224
Spring cleaning	225
Keeping track of finances	225
Worksheet #12: Stay on budget!	226
Taking care of yourself, and taking it in stride	229
Evaluate how things are going	230
Resources if things are going wrong	230
Don't forget where you came from	232
Wrapping it all up	232
Step 8: Coming home	**233**
Look in the mirror — you've changed	233

- What is reverse culture shock? 234
- Harder or easier? 235
- Home for a few days, for awhile, or forever? 235
- Who wants to hear a story? 235
- Stay exotic and 'international' 237
- Reconnecting and accepting drift 237
- Getting out vs. staying in 238
- Looking back and moving forward 238
- Adulting 239
- The worst-case scenario: you're home because you're broke 240
- Adopting a new home 240
- Networking and finding work 241
- If you're back for good… 242
- Leaving again might feel harder… or infinitely easier 243
- Wrapping it all up 243

What's next? 244
- Traveling philosophy 244
- Some pro-tips that didn't fit anywhere else 245
- Conclusions 246

Acknowledgements
This book is dedicated to you and your journey.

Thanks, as always, to Laura, my better half, an incredible woman, and ever-patient wife.

Thanks to Patricia Mackenzie for her intensive editing efforts on both editions.

Thanks for Sharon Gourlay at digitalnomadwannabe.com for an incredible forward.

Thanks to Tristan Kerr for a kick-ass book cover.

Thanks to Ricky Shetty for introducing me to some of the over 500 nomads he's interviewed on digitalnomadmastery.com.

Thanks to all the commenters on the early drafts, whose decades of combined travel and nomad experience make this book as informative as possible (alphabetized by family name):
- Laura Backe (AKA my wife)
- Myriam van Bavel (islasocial.com.au)
- Stephanie Berchiolly (careermakeoveracademy.com)
- Gianni Bianchini (nomadisbeautiful.com)
- Jennifer Booker Smith
- Mercè Maresma Casellas
- C.Angel Crush (facebook.com/groups/womenofamazon)
- Ina Danova
- Mariana Diaz Montiel (marianadiazmontiel.com)
- Nanouk van Gennip (samendewereldontdekken.nl)
- Ashley Grant (famousashleygrant.com)
- Ivana Greslikova (nomadisbeautiful.com)
- Candy Harrington (emerginghorizons.com)

- Tiraya Krongvanich (ffyre.net)
- Ian Hamshaw
- Nancie McKinnon (budgettravelerssandbox.com)
- Sandra Muller (sandralmuller.com)
- Dina Pelletier, MPH (globalcitizen.online)
- Cristina Puscas (prinarad.info)
- Susan Renner-Eggleston (luxurycolumnist.com)
- Toby Richardson (travellingminimalist.com)
- Jan Robinson (budgettraveltalk.com)
- Paul Ryken (minimalistjourneys.com)

Thanks to everyone who offered to share their 'becoming a nomad' story. You'll find several of them in the introduction, but you can see them all at becomingadigitalnomad.com/stories. You'll also find plenty of examples of the diversity of nomads over at becomingadigitalnomad.com/yes-you-can.

Foreword by Sharon Gourlay

Rewind five years.

I was a stay at home mum, studying part time and wishing my life was different. My husband seemed to be at work all the time, we barely made ends meet and my two toddlers drove me crazy. I missed the travel and opportunities I used to have and I couldn't help but think that there must be a better way.

Around the same time, I started reading family travel blogs. They didn't just show me that it was possible to travel with toddlers but I came across many where the families were digital nomads – traveling full time while they worked from their laptops.

To say I was jealous is an understatement. I wanted their lives so bad, yet I kept making excuses about why they could do it and I couldn't.

Their jobs transferred easily to online.

They already had a successful business so it was easy for them.

They got lucky.

You name an excuse, I thought it.

One day, however, I woke up and realised that the only difference between me and the people in these blogs is that *they took the chance*.

Sure, the occasional one may have had an advantage, but the majority were just like me. That is, if I also took the chance and went all in with this dream to become a digital nomad.

From that moment on, I decided *no more excuses*.

If other people could do it, so could I. I kept telling myself this as I announced to the world that I was going to be a digital nomad, even though at that point I still had no idea how.

Because I had realised the true "secret" to transforming your life – you can make your life whatever you want it to be as long as you are 100% in.

Instead of using my kids as an excuse, I used them as my driving force. I wanted a better life for all of us – one where there was far more pleasure and far less work. I wanted them to grow up with two parents present and as global citizens.

My digital nomad dream was born.

It's been an interesting journey to get from that moment of clarity that I was going to make it happen to making it happen. I spent the next year working on becoming a professional travel blogger. I built other sites as well, and, a year later, despite not having made much money, we left Australia indefinitely with the plan to grow my business and live life how we wanted.

I found there is nothing like going all in to make it happen and, immediately after leaving our home in Australia, we were making enough money to support us. A year later, we had cracked the five-figure per month mark. All thanks to travel blogging and affiliate marketing.

Today, we live where want, we work as much (or as little) as we want and we have freedom and flexibility that's not ruled by money or jobs.

There's been laughter, joy and extreme happiness. But there have also been tears, sadness, frustration and a lot of hard work. It's not been a straight journey from A to B but rather one with lots of curves and backward steps. However, it's also been the best journey of my life and I would not change a minute of it for anything.

Of course, being committed to changing your life and becoming a digital nomad is only the first step of the journey. There is so much to work out from how you will live to how you will make a living. It's easy to get overwhelmed and my best piece of advice is to take it one step at a time. *Solve one issue before you move on to the next*. And be confident that you can work it all out.

This book makes it easy to work your way through all the potential minefields in your way. I recommend you work through each chapter and complete the worksheets even if you think they don't apply to you. You may find out something interesting about yourself and how to make this journey work for you. This is especially the case with step 1 and you should spend some time answering all the questions and being clear on what you want your life to look like as this will feed into the rest of the process.

For example, when it came to how to make money, I knew my goals for becoming a digital nomad were all about lifestyle – I wanted to work less. So I concentrated on ways to earn money that were largely passive so I wasn't continually exchanging money for time. I did this via blogging, SEO and affiliate marketing. If I hadn't been clear on this, I may have worked as a freelancer instead which would not have led to a successful digital nomad experience for me.

Since starting my own journey, I have met so many digital nomads from all walks of life and backgrounds who have been able to make this lifestyle work. Chris Backe is one of these nomads.

I first met Chris about a month after I officially became a digital nomad. We met in Ao Nang in Southern Thailand. It was only the second time I had met someone in real life that was living the dream I wanted so much. What struck me about him was his determination and the different ways he was approaching making an online income. He seemed like he had been doing it for years. I was able to learn a lot from Chris and I am sure you will also be able to in this book.

If I can give you one final tip, it's to give the processes described in this book time. It takes time to find a way to make money that works for you. It takes time to work out how to make the digital nomad lifestyle work for you from the types of places you enjoy living to how long to spend in a place. Everyone is different and you need to find the right fit for you.

And finally, enjoy the ride! It's likely to be the most amazing one you have ever taken.

Sharon Gourlay
DigitalNomadWannabe.com

Notes from writing the 3rd edition

After being a digital nomad for almost seven years, it's easy to forget how out-of-the-ordinary the digital nomad lifestyle is. It's not just about the traveling or sightseeing, mind you — it's about any number of things. Over time, you have to stop and take stock of where life has taken you.

Where has life taken me in the past year?
- To Athens, Greece, where my wife and I rang in the new year.
- To Istanbul, Turkey, where we did some sightseeing and I playtested the games I'm working on.
- To Beirut, Lebanon, for a look at a lesser-traveled city.
- To Tbilisi, Georgia, where I'm pretty sure I gained a bit of weight from all the excellent food and drink.
- To Birmingham, England, for one of the largest board game conventions in Europe.
- To Baku, Azerbaijan, for another lesser-traveled city.
- To Tallinn, Estonia, for a look at a country that could be part of Northern Europe, Western Europe, or Eastern Europe.
- To Latvia and Lithuania, on a long weekend road trip from Estonia.
- To Lisbon, Portugal, for a glimpse into centuries of history.
- To a transatlantic repositioning cruise as an alternative to flying.
- To Canada for a wedding in my wife's family.
- To Essen, Germany, for the largest board game convention in the world.
- To Kyiv, Ukraine, as a return to Eastern Europe to ring in 2020.

Few of these would be considered digital nomad hotspots, and they don't need to be. Part of becoming a digital nomad is charting your own course, not blindly buying one-way tickets to popular places. You can be a digital nomad from just about anywhere in the world — so why this place or that place? **Go where you want!**

This 3rd edition, updated for 2020, updates hundreds of things throughout the book and adds new resources. Whether you're reading this book for the first time or the 20th, there's plenty to dig into here.

Intro

In a way, we have a rocket scientist to thank for the digital nomad lifestyle today.

In 1972, former NASA engineer Jack Nilles was permitted to work from home on a complex NASA communication system. People asked how he could be working when he was at home, and his response, *telecommuting*, quickly became a well-known term. Later, he began to research telecommuting and teleworking at the University of Southern California, and was the lead author of the seminal book, *The Telecommunications - Transportation Tradeoff*.

It proposed telecommuting as an 'alternative to transportation', and since it would reduce the number of commuters, it could solve issues like gridlock, long commutes to work, and potentially helping the national energy crisis the US was experiencing at the time. While the internet and the personal computer as we know them didn't yet exist, the authors predicted new technologies would emerge that would be as revolutionary to life as the automobile.

The freedom finder

This is Jane. Jane left school at 16 and got married at 20. Work, a family and 'normal' life followed but after 25 years she ran away from her marriage. Needing time away after a long drawn out divorce process, she resigned from her job and set off for Peru. Initially planning to be away for 7 months, she quickly realised that she never wanted to lose the sense of freedom that she was finally experiencing. Jane discovered that she was also inspiring others to believe in themselves again via her blog and so she began to support people as a personal

freedom mentor. Five years on, Jane is still travelling. See what Jane is up to now to at scarletjonestravels.com.

Find more nomad stories at becomingadigitalnomad.com/stories.

Another very early example of telecommuting and working with computers while away from the office comes from 1973. According to a January 1974 *Cycle World* article, a series of cassette tapes, phone adapters, and plastic time cards were used to time the ISDT, a six-day motorcycle endurance race held in the Berkshire Hills in Massachusetts. (Computers had been used in previous events, but only for backups, or they had created a lot of problems.) After riders had checked in, the worker would call the computer center and replay the tape, passing data to a computer in Michigan for compilation at a then state-of-the-art 75 baud, or bits per second.

Fast forward to December 1997, when a book by Hitachi executive Tsugio Makimoto and *Electronics Weekly* writer David Manners was released. It prophesied that smaller and more powerful computer chips, along with new mobile devices and greater internet connectivity, would lead to a revolution in how people worked, lived, and traveled.

The title: *Digital Nomads*.

Despite the extensive experience of both these authors, and although the book came from a well-known UK publisher, it was virtually ignored by the public. Maybe it was just ahead of its time, or perhaps people were too caught up in the dot-com boom. Whatever the case, it accurately predicted the future lifestyle and foresaw the technological shift that was coming.

Before the 20th century ended, a few more building blocks were put in place that made the digital nomad lifestyle technically possible. Paypal launched in 1998, making it possible for people to get paid without a bank account, and laptops began offering wi-fi in 1999. Elance (now Upwork) was also launched in 1999, and was one of the earliest places to make money as a freelancer online. Still, this was an exceptionally early time to be a digital nomad.

The marketing professional

This is James. After several years of working as an online marketing professional, James decided to take the plunge and freelance. James decided staying in the UK made little sense from a quality of life and financial standpoint, so James and his girlfriend became digital nomads. Over five years later, they're still on the road, and have lived in France, Spain, Portugal, Germany, and South Africa. Today, James continues to work as a marketing consultant. See where James is today at his travel lifestyle blog thistravelguide.com.

Find more nomad stories at becomingadigitalnomad.com/stories.

The concept of living and working wherever you like resurfaced in the mainstream in Tim Ferriss' 2007 best-selling book *The 4-Hour Workweek*, which promised a way to "escape the 9-5, live anywhere, and join the new rich". Also released in 2007: Apple's first iPhone, a category-defining device that offered mere mortals the chance to compute from virtually anywhere in the world. Between the 2007-2008 financial crisis and the realization that a better way to live and work may exist, the 'digital nomad' lifestyle gradually gained mainstream acceptance. Even the United States federal government employed over 100,000 remote workers in 2009, the same year National Geographic also started a 'Digital Nomad' blog.

More tools made remote work easier to start and find. Skype and Google Adsense started in 2003, while Facebook and

Twitter became available to everyone in 2006. People began leaving six-figure jobs and booking one-way flights to faraway countries to begin a new life — one where showing up to an office job became less important than actually doing good work, wherever they might be.

The writing movie-maker

This is Jason. In college he caught the filmmaking bug. After graduating, he moved to New York City and worked on some independent films, only to have a major project fall apart. He bounced back by finding a job with Lehman Brothers. He quickly became one of the top sales executives in his department. This afforded him the ability to produce a silly zombie movie, that he sold on Amazon. With no warning Lehman Brothers declared bankruptcy in 2008, leaving Jason out of a job. Jason started a blog on filmmaking. Eventually he created his first info product, started doing speaking gigs, wrote a 'traditional' book, and parlayed that experience into an executive position with a Hollywood film distribution company. See where Jason is today at jasonbrubaker.com.

Find more nomad stories at becomingadigitalnomad.com/stories.

The notion of 'remote work' or 'virtual workforces' continued to gain momentum. In 2012, a Gallup poll showed 39% of American workers did at least some of their work remotely during the year. Newspapers and magazines ran profiles of digital nomads alongside articles on how to talk to your boss about working remotely. A 2014 survey by Upwork found 79% of digital nomads planned to stay a digital nomad for the rest of their lives. Other surveys show remote workers to be more productive, have lower stress levels, better morale, reduced turnover, and on average, have a higher income.

Some digital nomads began keeping blogs, writing books, or running conferences and workshops on how to become a digital nomad. A cruise dedicated to nomads launched in 2015, and one famous nomad (Pieter Levels, of Nomadlist and other businesses) has predicted there will be one billion digital nomads by 2035 (levels.io/future-of-digital-nomads). Thailand officially launched a 'digital nomad visa' in 2017 that allows nomads to reside there for up to four years.

As of January 2018, Romania has made it legal for traditional, salaried employees to work remotely. Also, private health insurance can be purchased without having the public / state insurance — just a couple of baby steps towards enabling workers to work for whom they choose. In February 2018, another Upwork-commissioned survey found that 63% of American companies have remote workers, while 48% of companies use freelancers. That same month, Buffer's first State of Remote Work report found 90% of remote workers surveyed plan to work remotely for the rest of their career. Once you leave the office, it seems, it's hard to want to go back.

Thanks to the perfect storm of non-traditional needs and a disposable income, digital nomads have grown to become a niche market and industry. In mid-2018, Tortuga Backpacks introduced the Homebase Collection, a two-piece line of luggage specifically made for digital nomads — a backpack for everyday use and a waterproof duffel bag, presented as a modern-day take on the classic trunk. ("Traveling as a digital nomad is entirely different than traveling for a vacation, and therefore luggage for digital nomads should be designed differently than luggage for a vacation," says the blog post that launched the offering — along with notes about their year-long product testing with full-time nomads.) In May 2018, Vermont passed into a law a program that would attract digital nomads to their state with cash, and in mid-November 2018, Tulsa announced an initiative to offer cash, a subsidized apartment, and free office space to digital nomads that agreed to live in Tulsa (see it at tulsaremote.com).

In 2019, members of 'Generation Z' (born between 1995 and 2015) started becoming digital nomads, and Baby Boomers (born between 1946 and 1964) began to be tempted by remote work. Including 'Generation X' and the Millennials, this makes four generations of remote workers and digital nomads. A number of articles talked about the downsides of the lifestyle: the potential for loneliness, being disconnected from friends and family, and finding it difficult to establish a sense of community and identity.

With that said, the digital nomad lifestyle is ubiquitous, growing, and getting better. Estonia now has a digital nomad visa available, and the world's first 'digital nomad town' opened in Italy. Malaysia is making plans to offer a digital freelancing visa. A few places in the US now offer up to $10,000 for remote workers to settle in their areas — Vermont and Tulsa, Oklahoma are just two examples.

Connecting with other digital nomads means turning to social networks — r/digitalnomad on Reddit has over 550,000 subscribers, while several digital nomad groups on Facebook have tens of thousands of members. Facebook also holds plenty of niche groups for digital nomads, including some specifically for women (Female Digital Nomads has over 56,000 members), the LGBTQ community, vegans, and in virtually every major city on the planet.

But I couldn't be a nomad! I'm [insert reason here]. This book aims to make the digital nomad lifestyle as accessible as possible, no matter where you're from, your gender, the color of your skin, your sexual identity or preference, your age, your marital status, your religion, and so on. Odds are very good that there's someone like you already making it work — to see the list, head to becomingadigitalnomad.com/yes-you-can.

What is a digital nomad?

The BBC has called digital nomads "professionals who work online and therefore don't need to tie themselves to one particular office, city, or even country." It is, in many ways, a rewiring of the fabric of how life is for the majority of people. Ask 100 nomads *why* they do it, however, and you'll hear 100 different answers. Some will get philosophical about how being a nomad equals having the freedom to live. Some focus on their work, while others focus on their income streams. Still others start by mentioning where they live, where they've lived, and perhaps where they're going next. This is a classic example of what happens when each person defines their adventure for themselves instead of going off of some rigid, prescribed definition. A digital nomad may well be answering the question, **What would your life look like if you could freely chase what you want, without limitations?**

The traveling bookkeeper

This is Anna. Anna studied four different degrees in Tourism and Business with the goal of working and traveling around the world. She tried many jobs but none of them offered really the travel experience she really wanted. During a company trip to Turkey, she only saw the airport and the supplier's office, and finally decided to quit as a result. Anna decided it was time to really travel and see the world the way she wanted! Anna started as a content writer for travel-related websites and offering proofreading in Spanish. In 2017, she started

writing her own blog about her travels and the life of a digital nomad in Spanish. See where Anna is today at latravelista.com.

Find more nomad stories at becomingadigitalnomad.com/stories.

Here's the definition I'll use throughout the book: **a digital nomad is a person who lives nomadically (or travels at will) and works digitally while traveling**. Since this is still such a new way of working and living, there's more than one term that tries to address it. 'Telecommuting' and 'teleworking' were commonly used during the 1980's and 1990's, but today they feel like relics from those eras. 'Lifestyle design' addresses how one might *live*, but it says nothing about how one *works*. 'Remote work' addresses how one might *work* while traveling, but it says nothing about how one *lives*. 'Location Independent', a term coined by Lea Jovy (née Woodward), works for some people since it implies they travel and work. While I acknowledge the term 'digital nomad' is a cliché to some, it best encompasses both sides of how one lives and works.

A digital nomad lives nomadically — traveling as they like, where they like, for an unfixed amount of time. Some nomads will choose to travel for a part of the year, then use an apartment or house as a base for the rest of the year. They need not be constantly traveling to be nevertheless thinking about and planning their next stop, their next trip, and so on.

A digital nomad works digitally — meaning your work and money-making endeavors are typically done or found on your computer and through an internet connection. They're not usually tied to your physical location, though some gigs might be.

The Singaporean copywriter

This is Crunch. Born in Singapore, Crunch graduated with a double degree in Business and Political Science in 2012. Everyone expected her to land a cushy job, but Crunch had always dreamed of traveling the world, exploring new places, and meeting new people. In 2014, she quit her job, bought a one-way ticket to South America, and taught English for a year before starting her digital nomad career as a freelance copywriter. Crunch is making her way around Asia while working anywhere between 30 minutes and 3 hours a day to support her travel habits. See what Crunch is up to now at lovechildoftheworld.wordpress.com.

Find more nomad stories at becomingadigitalnomad.com/stories.

Although 'digital nomad' is the term I'll use in the book, don't let the term be a hang-up.
There are debates about whether a person that 'only' travels three or six months a year is a digital nomad, or whether they may call themselves a digital nomad. **The important thing to remember: it's not about how much you travel, how fast you travel, or how many countries you visit.** Use the term you want to find community, not to divide.

The family that travels together...

The Mulder Family lived the normal suburban life, but they wanted more time with their kids and less time sitting at an office desk. They decided to take the leap. Sold their house, quit their jobs, bought an RV and started traveling through Europe. It took hard work and full dedication, but now, years after they left, they have a successful business. Because they keep their costs down, they're able to work part-time and live comfortably. See what they're up to now at digitalnomadwithkids.com.

Find more nomad stories at becomingadigitalnomad.com/stories.

Digital nomads have become a testing ground for a radical question: **What happens when people view the world (not just a city or a country) as their home?** After all, people have seen taxes rise, benefits cut, house prices explode, incentives to own things decline, and traditions cast aside, so it seems only natural for them to openly wonder *'Why should I stay put?'* or *'What would happen if I chose experiences over materialism?'*

Digital nomads have a very different relationship with other aspects of their life, starting with what feels normal to them. For most people, getting up, commuting to work, working, commuting home, and going on a short vacation is normal to them. Becoming comfortable with what *they* define as 'normal' is an important part of the transition.

This is possible because of the information era we live in. The pattern of life is quickly changing as well, and the notions of getting married, getting a good job, having kids, and/or buying a house are no longer universal goals. The world has also changed dramatically — machines and automation do a lot of the jobs humans might have done decades ago. Today's jobs don't necessarily require working with colleagues in the same physical office, which opens the door for different time zones and locations to come into play. A person about to leave for the day in, say, Seattle, can pass on some work to their digital nomad colleague in, say, Thailand. The colleague in Thailand does their part during their work shift, then sends it back before Seattle wakes up. The digital nomad lifestyle still requires *collaboration*, of course, but it need not be in the same place or at the same time.

Different places you travel to can affect your health. Wake up in Los Angeles and you're breathing some of the highest levels of particle pollution in the US. Just because you suffer from a specific malady doesn't mean it'll continue in a new country, however. Something in the local air, food, or water might cause your acne to flare up or you to cough for one reason or another. More than a few digital nomads have discovered what they thought was an allergy was just an issue that disappeared as soon as they left. In case you needed another reason to travel, here you go.

For some digital nomads, leaving their home country also means escaping the control their government has had on them. Choosing to live outside your home country limits how much influence that government has on your life, and is a way of taking back control.

What digital nomads *are*

Digital nomads are making a choice to be in control. This lifestyle is one that's *actively chosen*. It requires contemplation, reflection, but most importantly, it requires the truth. You can lie to yourself about what you think you want or what you think will make you happy… but you can't outrun any internal demons. Some of the many choices you can make:
- Would you rather sleep in and do your work in the evenings, or stick to a 9-to-5 type of schedule?
- Would you rather live near a beach, an ocean, a forest, or in a 47th story apartment?
- Do you want to spend more time with your kids, your spouse / life partner, your friends, or head out on your own?
- Do you want to more thoroughly explore your religion / spirituality, or start a life without the religion / spirituality you grew up with?
- Do you want to embrace the many communities around you, or would you prefer to live a less communal life?

Digital nomads are of every shape, color, age, marital status and 'type'. Forget what you think you know — nomads are 18 to 80 years old (and older!), male, female, white, black, brown, yellow, single, married, childless, with children, pregnant, gay, straight, trans, religious, atheist, agnostic, conservative, liberal, non-political, high school dropouts, college graduates, and so on.

The traveling bookkeeper

This is Susan. Susan worked for others for years, but wanted more freedom and better wages. In 2008, Susan started her own bookkeeping business in Austin, Texas. She developed a steady clientele, working onsite at her clients' offices, but still

took frequent vacations to feel free. In 2014, she developed a plan, worked out all the technical requirements to work remotely, and become a digital nomad. She approached her clients with the proposal to work remotely rather than onsite. Happily, most of them said yes. Since late September 2015, Susan has logged over 30,000 miles exploring the USA and Canada as a digital nomad. See where Susan is now at SoloTripsAndTips.com.

Find more nomad stories at becomingadigitalnomad.com/stories.

Digital nomads use their online presence to craft their offline life. Whether you're joining Facebook groups or perusing events on Meetup, you'll likely learn of events happening online. One does not live solely online, of course — needing to catch up and meet people in real life remains important.

Digital nomads view and work with money differently. This lifestyle challenges your relationship with and preconceptions about money. Some nomads discover just how cheaply they can live and get by, while others aim to make enough money so they can live as lavishly as they want, anywhere they choose. Either way, money and material things are no longer the way to keep score — having the time and mobility to live the way you want is. Money is just a tool to help nomads do the things they want — saving money is still important, but so is spending it on the things that matter to you. You are not 'rich' just because you make a ton of money, you're rich because you have the choices and freedom to live as you like.

Along these same lines, digital nomads usually choose to live with less. It doesn't *have* to mean living out of a suitcase or sacrificing the things you want in your life, but it's difficult to own a lot of things with this mobile lifestyle. I have two things to say to that: First, if there's something that's really important to your lifestyle, there's a very good chance you'll find it — or an excellent substitute — wherever it is you're going. Second, it's worth asking what's truly a deal-breaker in your mind. *Must you travel with 12 pairs of shoes, or can you manage with only three pairs (or, better, only one or two)?* More of something is not necessarily better. There's a lot less 'keeping up with the Joneses' with nomads than you might think, and using material things to compare supposed success goes out of style real quick.

The multilingual couple

This is Ivana and Gianni. They lived in Frankfurt, Germany, had stable jobs, a great community of friends, and a regular salary. Ivana and Gianni felt they were sacrificing our dreams for the feeling of social security, economic stability and a comfortable but limited way of living. They decided they were going to quit smoking in 2012, and if they could quit for a year, they'd hit the road. The motivation was strong, and they did it! Ivana and Gianni took a year or so to save some money, then bought a one way ticket to Bangkok and never looked back. Currently they're running the travel website Nomad is Beautiful and blog in their own languages, Italian and Slovak, while venturing around the globe with two carry-on backpacks. See where Ivana and Gianni are now at nomadisbeautiful.com.

Find more nomad stories at becomingadigitalnomad.com/stories.

What digital nomads are *not*

- **Digital nomads are not lazy.** 'Lazy' is when you fail to stand up for your beliefs or interests and just let life happen to you. 'Lazy' is what happens when you just follow the path of least resistance. Nomads take on a lot more challenges than the average human, and those challenges only get harder when your lifestyle goes against the flow or the mainstream way. Focusing on more meaningful work and shying away from busywork (or 'work for the sake of work') means there's more time to be productive and do the things you want. Also, contrary to the popular stereotype, few nomads *actually* work at the beach — it can be difficult to get comfortable, and then there's the sand, the water, the salty air to deal with...
- **Digital nomads are not running away from their problems.** Yes, there are people that think leaving the country or quitting their job will solve their problems. Granted, quitting a toxic job or getting away from unhealthy co-workers can help, but some problems won't go away just because you quit a job or change countries. Wherever you go, so does whatever internal drama or issues you're dealing with. If you don't deal with these issues, they'll continue to drain your energy and awareness no matter where you go.
- **Digital nomads are not kids who chose not to grow up.** The concept of becoming a nomad can look like one is suffering from 'Peter Pan syndrome.' What is 'growing up,' though? Taking care of oneself? Buying real estate? Getting married? Making babies? Digital nomads may choose to do all of these things... or none of them. Nomads may not follow the traditional or typical timeline, but then, such timelines are simply social constructs or expectations — and have little, if anything at all, to do with actually 'growing up.'

The traveling freelancer

This is Aleah. She had a full-time job as a counselor when she started working as a part-time editor and proofreader online. She took on one or two projects at a time, editing books or ebooks, advertising materials, and even blog posts. The pay wasn't great at first, but after 2 years, she was already earning as much as her full-time job. She needed a break from her work, and also had a travel blog that was getting some attention, so she decided to quit her job and travel. Follow Aleah's adventures at solitarywanderer.com.

Questions you've had about digital nomads but were afraid to ask

Do I have to constantly be on the move or always going somewhere new? Nope. Some digital nomads settle into a routine of spending, say, the summer in one country or the winter in another place (either to avoid the colder weather or to enjoy it!), and so on. Others will look to get residency in a country of their choice so they can stay for longer periods of time. While the term 'nomad' is used, the notion is that you're free to move when, how, and where you choose.

Do I have to be around people all the time? I'm kind of an introvert [or] ***I don't like being in large groups...*** Simple answer: no. The thing with digital nomads is that you're in charge of creating your own network or community. Where and how you do that is totally up to you. I recommend finding the local networking spaces to connect with other nomads, whether they're online or offline. A good question to ask: what do I want to get as a result of connecting with this group? Simply socializing and having a beer is a great answer. Finding a partner for a new project is another great answer. Knowing what you want before you arrive gives that networking time some structure and purpose.

Do I have to be entrepreneurial? In some ways, yes. As a digital nomad, you might prefer not having a boss or someone always watching over you. In some cases, your traditional job might travel with you, so you still have a regular salary and familiar responsibilities. In other cases, you might quit the job you have to take another job that's more remote-worker friendly.

Do I have to be super-tech-savvy? No, but technology will play a larger role in your life than it might right now. If you're working online, this will mean mastering new skills or online tools to create and deliver your work. You'll socialize more online and spend time researching the places you want to go, booking where you'll stay, or the like. Don't fear your computer — if you're not sure what it can do for you, take some classes or get a friend to teach you.

Do I have to go to Thailand? Absolutely not. In fact, if you're still on the fence about this whole thing and just want to give it a try, head to the next state, province, county, or city over (and be sure to read the Nomadus Interruptus section for the best way to test the lifestyle out). The goal here is to break away from what's familiar and find your own path. Some people choose Thailand because it's exotic and cheap, while others just follow the crowd there.

Do I have to leave my pet(s) behind? No, but they do add some extra considerations and research time. You'll want to ensure their paperwork is in order and research to know what treatments are needed, and when.

Can I be just a part-time nomad? Absolutely! Part-time nomads choose to spend some months of the year as nomads and others at their home base. Whether it's circumstances, choices, or personal preferences, that choice is entirely plausible and yours to make.

Can I make money as a [insert your occupation / career here] once I become a nomad? Probably, but it depends. If your job *requires* you to be in the same room as someone or to physically touch the thing or person you're working with, it's going to be harder. You can certainly aim to take that knowledge you've accumulated and use that in different ways, though. Many, many things are delivered and created digitally — and as long as you have an internet connection, those digital creations can be received and sent anywhere on the planet.

Are digital nomads 'stable'? Yes, but in a different way from how people have traditionally lived. Let me use an analogy.

Imagine you're standing on a square piece of wood with a tall block under each corner. You're standing in the center of this square, and it feels very stable. This represents a typical, average life with a full-time job, a house, etc. Suddenly, someone thwacks away one of those blocks. You can still adjust and balance, of course — you just need to move and balance a bit. Now imagine another block gets thwacked away. That platform gets a lot more precarious.

Now imagine you're standing on the center of a seesaw, with one leg on either side. You can choose to keep the seesaw perfectly balanced and level, or you can push down on one side to make it hit the ground. It's you at the center, choosing how to balance (or unbalance things). You still have to be careful because you can fall forward or backward, of course, and you can't just completely zone out.

In the first example, those blocks might be things like your job, your family support, your friends, maybe even the support a government offers its citizens. If you lose your job — thwack! — there goes that block. You can adjust, but you might not feel stable until the block is put back in place. In the second example, your being in the center means you can push down on one side — say, work — and spend your time doing that.

Is it worth it? It sounds like a lot of work... It is, and it is. The digital nomad lifestyle is not one that rewards just sitting back and waiting for things to happen. If you do that in your hometown, you'll find you just sort of drift by and accept whatever life hands you. If you do that as a nomad, you can find yourself in a bad way fast.

Think about where you want to be a year from now — it's not an exaggeration to say you can be living on a different continent, at a different job, making new friends, learning new skills, speaking a new language, doing something you're truly passionate about, and creating an entirely new life for yourself.

How to use this book

This book will guide you through a step-by-step process to transition into — or just test out — the digital nomad lifestyle. As you're reading, you will come across a number of worksheets throughout the book. The top of each worksheet will have a link to a PDF you can print and fill out offline, or a form you can fill out online. Either way, you may save or print these as you like. The forms are completely anonymous and never ask for any identifying information.

Most books about the digital nomad lifestyle don't even mention the possibility of testing out the lifestyle, but we're going to take an entire section to discuss that. Look for that in the Nomadus Interruptus section. Think of this testing process like how you might approach dating — whether you get introduced to people by friends or you try your luck with online dating, you start carefully. You get to know the person. You ask about their background, their beliefs, the future, what they want out of a relationship, and so on. If all indications are a go, you go on a second or third date and begin to ask deeper questions. You figure out how comfortable you feel around them, whether you can trust them. However you approach dating, think of that as a parallel to your digital nomad journey.

Why should I do a test? Why not just go? I'd much rather see you test it out and discover it isn't for you than to buy a one-way ticket to Thailand and then realize it's not for you. Don't sell your car or donate your furniture until you're ready to commit to this lifestyle. Learn, ask questions, and make some room in your life for the changes you want to make.

While you're working your way through this book, one overarching mindset stands above all: **you need to do the work yourself**. You must also accept and embrace the unknown as part of the experience. No place, even in today's era of Google Street Maps and millions of Tripadvisor reviews, is completely knowable. Furthermore, no lifestyle should be expected to provide all the answers for you — ultimately, in this as in every other facet of your life, your choices and mindset determine where life takes you.

Next, a warning: there are more than a few programs or systems out there that will set you up with a place to live, a built-in social network, and so on. It's not the *program* that's problematic, it's the *mindset* of 'we'll take care of all your needs' that makes them tough to recommend. Their incentive is to keep you in the program month after month, not teach you how to connect with locals, find work, or the sort of things that help you become an *independent* nomad. There are no tricks, no get-rich-quick schemes, and no program that will make you a nomad. I promise this will take some serious, hard work — and that it will be worth it.

That's not to say you can't take or follow advice from others. Even after a decade of living abroad, I've found there's always someone who has more knowledge than I do on a given topic. I'll happily ask questions on Facebook groups or reach out to people to learn what they know, but there's a big difference between asking for advice and relying on someone else to do the hard work for you.

Experience and perspective — about the author and contributors

After graduating from college with a Bachelor of Science in Business in 2004, I worked at a Radio Shack, a mattress store, as an accountant, as a newspaper deliverer, and as a teacher of computer classes. It's not exactly a glowing resume by any stretch, but it was enough to prove to myself I didn't really fit a lot of typical jobs. I left the USA on March 22, 2008 to start a job teaching English in South Korea. For about five years, I taught English in South Korea, traveled throughout the country, wrote a blog about travel and life in South Korea, and met a girl. After weekend-long dates traveling the country,

Laura and I got married in 2013, just before we left Korea, and we've lived together as nomads ever since.

As nomads, we have spent two years in Thailand, three months traveling across Western Europe, about nine months in South America (Colombia, Ecuador, and Peru), about a year in the US and Canada (primarily on an epic 17,000km road trip from Nova Scotia to Key West, Florida — and back along a different route), and all over Eastern Europe for the last few years. During all that time, I've been a travel blogger, an author, an editor, a proofreader, a photographer, a web developer, a book reviewer, an English teacher, and a board game designer.

This book isn't just about my experience, though. Dozens of other digital nomads of various genders, colors, and nationalities had a hand in making this the best possible resource to humans of all kinds.

The passionate environmentalist

This is Joseph. Joseph studied journalism in the UK, but felt that he couldn't make positive global change working in the press. Having eco-volunteered in Portugal, Albania and Italy whilst studying, he graduated and began working in the environmental industry. In 2015, his digital nomad adventure began, with his eco-friendly employer granting permission to work abroad in Spain and Portugal. He returned to the UK a few months later to create a plan to generate his own income, set his own hours, and work wherever he wanted. He launched his Environmental Copywriting Agency in February 2016, and Joseph has been living and working in Spain, Portugal, Morocco, Thailand, and the Czech Republic.

Joseph says that his home is where his Macbook is, and that moving back to the UK is an unthinkable task. See what Joseph does at cpath.co.uk.

Find more nomad stories at becomingadigitalnomad.com/stories.

Is this the right time to become a nomad?

This can be asked a couple of different ways: when's the perfect time for me to become a digital nomad? Is this a good time to make a big change?

A couple of thought processes are at play here. There are certainly obligations you might have to fulfill first, but don't let obligations cause you to wait until everything is perfect. The time will never be 'perfect,' just like the traffic lights will never be green all at the same time, but there are probably signs it's the *right* time. Who might be sending those signs? Your family, your job, your friends, or maybe even the universe itself.

The three most common times people begin to consider the nomad lifestyle are:
- A traumatic event
- Completing a major milestone
- After a sudden realization or epiphany

You may have heard the famous quote by the writer Anaïs Nin (even if it isn't always attributed to her): "And the time came when the risk to remain tight in a bud was more painful than the risk it took to blossom." For some people, a traumatic event sparks the first internal debate — getting fired from their job, health issues, breaking up with a boyfriend or girlfriend, a divorce, etc. Such events will make almost anybody re-evaluate core aspects of their life, and it is now that they're often more willing to take more risks and consider options they might never have thought of.

In other cases, completing a major milestone means you're suddenly free to consider new options. This might be university, military service, or something else. A lot of time and energy has been devoted to something, but now you might be asking 'what's next?'. If the traditional answers are less than satisfying, this might open the door to considering new options.

In still other cases, there's a sudden realization or epiphany that causes you to reconsider where you are in life. It might be a friend posting a beach picture on Facebook or a casual conversation with someone you haven't talked to awhile. A random question, pondered on a random Tuesday afternoon, may be the thing that prompts more questions and research.

As you're beginning to put your own puzzle pieces together, you may realize that what you really want out of life has changed. Your choices can always change, of course — there are no long-term commitments or contracts with the digital nomad lifestyle. Maybe you'll find yourself getting bored of living near the beach (*yes, this really does happen to some people!*), or your evolving interests make you want to go somewhere new. That's totally fine! Instead of asking '*What do I want?*', try to focus on '*What would excite me?*'. You're about to have the **whole world** at your fingertips to help you find your bliss. If that doesn't get your heart beating a little faster, it might be time to check your pulse. To 'be realistic' is not advice you'll find in this book — there's no reason to limit yourself like that.

The family life
Say hi to The Wilson's: Tim, Yunche, Jordyn (age 7) and Aria (age 4). After years of chasing the American dream, going through a bankruptcy. and losing their home along with everything they worked so hard for, the Wilson's decided it was time for a massive change. They sold everything they had left, bought some one-way tickets, and started a travel adventure around the world. In July 2018, they set up a homebase in Chiang Mai, Thailand where they will continue to travel the world and worldschool their girls. Learn more about the Wilson's at wanderlustfamilylife.com.

Find more nomad stories at becomingadigitalnomad.com/stories.

Eight steps to becoming a digital nomad (and an interim section)

These eight steps are meant to be read and accomplished in order, but you're welcome to read ahead.

Step 1: Know yourself and what you want focuses entirely on *you*, good reader. Let's understand the person you see when you look in the mirror.

Step 2: Clarify your desires and acknowledge limitations does two important things in gearing you up for your journey.

Nomadus interruptus: Just a test, please is an interim section dedicated to setting up a good test of the digital nomad lifestyle.

Step 3: Making money puts together a comprehensive list of how digital nomads can make money, along with some notes on how to manage your money across borders.

Step 4: Get affairs in order focuses on what needs to be done before leaving your country.

Step 5: Gear up and slim down focuses on what to pack and how to deal with the rest of your stuff.

Step 6: The big move and settling in walks you through your last few days at your old place and your first few days at your new place.

Step 7: Start enjoying your new life helps you establish new habits, make new connections, and make your nomad lifestyle a sustainable one.

Step 8: Coming home focuses on creating a home for yourself, seeing your home country with more worldly eyes, and helps you deal with reverse culture shock.

Get help planning your journey

Many digital nomads have made this journey alone, but that doesn't mean you have to. Start by joining the Facebook group for this book at facebook.com/groups/becomingadigitalnomad and feel free to ask questions there.

If you're looking for more specialized assistance, I consult with people one-on-one via Skype to help plan your digital nomad journey. These one-hour individual sessions will help you to clarify your goals and manage your expectations, answer your questions, connect you to resources, and discuss any specific concerns you might have. Whatever step you're on in this digital nomad journey, a one-hour consultation can save you countless hours of potential mis-steps and uncertainty. See becomingadigitalnomad.com/digital-nomad-consulting for information on scheduling an appointment.

For now, let's get started on the first (and arguably the most important) step.

Step 1: know yourself and what you want

Like any major change in your life, knowing yourself and what you want to achieve when you make this change is paramount. Learning how to know yourself could easily be the subject of an entirely different book, but for the sake of argument, start by asking yourself some questions. Yes, I know this looks like a metric boatload of questions — many of which you may have never asked yourself before — but they're still important to consider.

Here's how to handle this section:
- Grab a pen and paper, or open a new note in Notepad or Evernote — however you like to take notes.
- Write or type your answer, starting with the number of the question (you don't have to copy the question). **Aim to freewrite or type in your stream of consciousness** — don't go back and edit your answers until you finish the section.
- If you prefer a worksheet, head to becomingadigitalnomad.com/worksheet1. You can print off the worksheet to fill out offline, or type your answers, then save or print a PDF of them.
- Be honest with yourself. There should be no secrets here, and no one needs to see your answers but you. Some of these are yes or no type questions, but I want you to go beyond a single word answer. Try starting your answer with 'yes, because…' or 'no, because…' to flesh out your answers beyond the basics.

Can't I just read through the book and skip the worksheets? Hey, you paid for it — use the resources here however you want. This book and the worksheets are put together for use in chronological order. Feel free to read the book all the way through, then return to the worksheets, if you think that will be the most helpful.

As mentioned in the introduction, this process we're about to explore is not unlike dating. When we go on a date, we carefully consider what we hope to find in a good match, we get to know them, we choose how to spend time with them, and so on. If it's a match, we take it to the next level.

One word of caution: this first worksheet is the longest in the book. Feel free to answer one section at a time if that's more your style.

Time for your first date!

Worksheet #1: know yourself

Date: _____

Find this at becomingadigitalnomad.com/worksheet1. Print a copy and complete offline, or complete online, then print or save.

For this first section, I want you to think just about you and no one else, whether or not you plan to travel with somebody. This isn't about your significant other, other family members, or your best friend. This is strictly about *you*.

1. Am I happy right now, or is something holding me back from being happy?
2. Where do I want to be a year from now?
3. What would a perfect day look like?
4. What would I change about my day-to-day life?
5. What do I feel is missing in my life?
6. What will keep me motivated through times of difficulty?
7. What's something I'd like to do, but I haven't had the time / energy to try?

Next, let's think about what you want.

8. If I could have or do anything I want, what would it be? Materialistic stuff? Bucket-list stuff? Experiences?
9. Why do I want these things?
10. Do I feel unhappy with the status quo, or have I felt 'stuck'?
11. When do I want to become a digital nomad? OR When would be the right time?
12. Am I waiting for something? Someone? Do I need to finish or complete something?
13. Assuming I can have it all, where do I fantasize about going? (Don't hold back! Any specific country? A city? A beach area? A certain culture or vibe? No limits here.)

14.   What about my current city / country do I like? Love? Hate? Be brutally honest. Love the open road? Hate public transportation? Is it polluted? Hard to do what I love?

Now, let's think about work — not just the physical place where you do the work, but the things you do for work itself.

15.   Where am I at in my career?
16.   What do I feel like I was put on earth to do?
17.   What jobs or gigs could I take that are similar to what I do now?
18.   What talents or skills of mine are going underused?
19.   (If currently employed) Can my job go with me? (If it doesn't require you to be at a specific physical location or to physically touch someone, it's a possibility)
20.   Is my business / company open to the notion of remote work / telecommuting? Are other people at my business telecommuting / remote working?

Next, let's consider other people we're connected to:

21.   Whose needs do I need to consider beyond my own?
22.   Who would my stakeholders and companions be? (Let's define stakeholders as people you trust to have your needs and desires at heart, while companions are people coming with you on this journey)
23.   What do my stakeholders and companions have to say?
24.   How will my becoming a digital nomad affect them?

Let's also think about the digital nomad lifestyle:

25.   Are any of my friends or family members currently digital nomads?
26.   What conceptions (or pre-conceptions) do I have about the digital nomad lifestyle?
27.   Is there anywhere I need to be in the next year (a friend's wedding, a family reunion, etc.)?
28.   Do I have some savings available?
29.   Am I able to leave town for long enough to test this lifestyle out?
30.   Do I have a passport?

Whether or not the digital nomad lifestyle is for you, this type of self-exploration is a chance to grow and learn about you.

Some important things to start working on: passports and visas

First things first: got your passport? It's not necessary if you're just testing out the nomad lifestyle elsewhere in your country, but it's *absolutely required* if you're going to do any sort of international traveling.

I already have a passport... Great! How old is it? Do you need to renew it? You need more than six months of validity (in other words, more than six months before it expires) just to arrive in most countries. Other countries don't want your passport to expire while you're there, in other words. If you don't have it yet, get started — it can take weeks or months depending on where you're from and their promised processing times. Most countries will have faster or expedited services available for extra fees as well.

- Americans, start at usa.gov/passport. Get the passport *book*, not the passport *card* (the card only allows travel around North America, and can't be used elsewhere).
- Australians, start at passports.gov.au/passportsexplained/pages/quicknewadultpassportguide.aspx. You'll need a guarantor / referee to vouch for you.
- Brits, start at gov.uk/apply-first-adult-passport. You will need a countersigner (someone that has known you for more than 2 years, has a passport already, and works in or is retired from a "recognised profession").

- Canadians, start at canada.ca/en/immigration-refugees-citizenship/services/canadian-passports/new-adult-passport.html.
- Irish, start at dfa.ie/passports-citizenship/how-to-apply-for-a-passport. You will need a witness (which can be a Garda from your Garda station or someone in one of about 20 other professions) to sign and stamp your application.
- Kiwis, start at passports.govt.nz/what-you-need-to-renew-or-apply-for-a-passport. You can apply online if you have a RealMe verified account, and you will need a referee.

Most countries have specific rules for passport photos, so find a place (or photo-taking machine) that specifically sells passport photos. There always seems to be at least a couple of places close to embassies or places where passport applications are accepted, but a quick Google search should find a suitable place. While some passport offices may have photo-taking machines or a photo service, don't expect or assume there will be one.

Quick pro-tip: once you have your passport, make some paper copies of it. Put one copy in each bag, ideally one in an external pocket *and* another in internal pocket of each bag. It helps to identify your bag if it's ever lost, and always gives you some ID in case other bags are lost.

What about visas? Whether you have your passport or are in the process of getting one, visas are the other half to being allowed into a country. A visa is essentially permission to enter and visit another country for a specific purpose, and is given by that country to you.

The good news: many countries will offer you entry into the country without a visa. Whether this is called visa-free travel, a visa waiver or a visa-on-arrival, no advance preparations are necessary. Just show up at airport immigration (you can't miss this since you can't avoid it), present your passport, and wait for the stamp. This is a privilege, not a right, and it's typically based on where your passport is from.

The bad news: *many* does not equal *all*. Each country makes their own visa rules and sets their own prices for the privilege for entering their country. While most countries will make it easy to be a tourist, the process to get another type of visa (e.g. business or educational) can range from easy to very difficult. Also, some passports are considered very powerful (e.g. they allow easy entrance to many countries), some passports are rather weak (e.g. they allow easy entrance to fewer countries).

Your country's embassy will have the most official information, but travisa.com has an easy-to-search source of unofficial information. Personally, any country that wants to make it challenging or expensive to get in is not (normally) a country we'll spend any time trying to enter. That applies to fewer and fewer countries these days, though.

Next up: it's time to ask what's important to you.

Worksheet #2: what's important to you?

Date: _____

Find this at becomingadigitalnomad.com/worksheet2. Print a copy and complete offline, or complete online, then print or save.

Circle / note how important each aspect is to you on a scale of 1 to 10 (1 = not important at all, 10 = the most important thing). If another adult will be joining you, have them circle / note their thoughts on a separate copy of this worksheet.

	Not important Very important
Being close to home	1 2 3 4 5 6 7 8 9 10
Climate / air quality	1 2 3 4 5 6 7 8 9 10
Comforts of home	1 2 3 4 5 6 7 8 9 10
English level	1 2 3 4 5 6 7 8 9 10
Exotic and exciting	1 2 3 4 5 6 7 8 9 10
Fast internet	1 2 3 4 5 6 7 8 9 10
Good food / drink	1 2 3 4 5 6 7 8 9 10
Having fun / nightlife	1 2 3 4 5 6 7 8 9 10
Lots of expats / nomads	1 2 3 4 5 6 7 8 9 10
Low cost of living	1 2 3 4 5 6 7 8 9 10
Physical accessibility	1 2 3 4 5 6 7 8 9 10
Safety	1 2 3 4 5 6 7 8 9 10

Of the 12 elements above, list the three most important to you in order:

The most important element to me is
_____, because _____ .

The second most important element to me is
_____, because _____ .

The third most important element to me is
_____, because _____ .

Some possible destinations

Worksheet #2 gave you a sense of what's important to you, so now we need to match those priorities with where to go. As part of knowing what you want, it's time to start researching your initial countries of choice. Start getting into the habit of keeping your ears open and learning about new places from your social media or news sources of choice.

This process can feel overwhelming at first — the world is a big place, after all, and there are plenty of places to check out. While there are no right or wrong answers, some places are definitely better than others for the first-time digital nomads. Several spots are well-known as hotspots for good reasons:

- **Bali, Indonesia** — while sometimes dismissed as a cliché, the strong Balinese culture combines nicely with a cheap cost of living. The internet is supposedly everywhere (though it's not always fast or reliable), as are the co-working spaces (we'll get to these later). Watch out for the traffic, don't bother trying to drive, and stay hydrated in the heat.
- **Bangkok, Thailand** — an excellent introduction to urban southeast Asian life. Since it's big, there's plenty of co-working spaces, international food, and networking to be had. Cheap massages, too. More than a few nomads have complained about it being hot and dirty… but that's Bangkok for you. Step inside a mall or a 7/11 for a blast of air-conditioning, but watch for scams.
- **Barcelona, Spain** — while the city is dealing with an over-tourism problem, Barcelona remains a beautiful urban hub to welcome you to the European Schengen Zone. Expect moderate weather and cheap wine but, being part of Western Europe, it's not the cheapest place to live.
- **Bucharest, Romania** — it's outside the Schengen Zone, it's about as cheap as Europe gets, and it has some very fast internet. It's also still a little rough around the edges. You can't judge the Communist-era buildings by their

exteriors, though — peek inside and you'll find plenty of modern touches. As elsewhere in Eastern Europe, many people under the age of 35 speak English well.
- **Budapest, Hungary** — Budapest is "a buzzing hub for expats / digital nomads", according to Cristina Puscas, and a hub of history and architecture as well. It's part of the Schengen Zone, but currently uses the forint (not the euro). Plenty of co-working spaces around.
- **Chiang Mai, Thailand** — the largest city in northern Thailand is arguably the epicenter of the digital nomad lifestyle. It's cheap, has plenty of places to work from, and offers a nice mix of modern and history. Protip: rent a scooter to get around town instead of worrying about where the *songthaews* will take you (always wear a helmet, naturally!).
- **Ho Chi Minh City (HCMC), Vietnam** — while crowded, chaotic, and full of traffic, the internet is fast, the coffee is great, and the street food "fantastic" according to Ivana Greslikova. "Da Nang is becoming a new digital nomad hub, too," she added. It's one of the cheapest places to live in the world, and visas for 6 or 12 months are fairly easy to get. Hanoi and Hue are worth a look as well.
- **Lisbon, Portugal** — while its location in the Schengen Zone may limit your stay to three months, it's considered one of the more affordable parts of Western Europe. The internet is fast, and its location near the coast makes it ideal if you're into water sports.
- **Medellin, Colombia** — the city formerly known as the murder capital and Pablo Escobar's headquarters is now one of the best introductions to South America you can find. Cheap, excellent food and beautiful weather make a powerful duo for anyone that might be on the fence. Knowing Spanish is helpful, but you can get by on English only. Protip: head to the Poblado neighborhood to party or eat well, but live elsewhere to get some of the local flavor.
- **Toronto, Canada** — the cultural capital is one of the most diverse cities in North America. The climate and higher cost of living might make this a less desirable choice for some, but it's a fun city with lots of opportunities to connect

with locals. Consider Scarborough and Mississauga as two other cities connected to the Greater Toronto Area, or GTA.

A quick note: All the places above are urban centers / cities, but some nomads prefer living or traveling in more rural areas for a variety of reasons. As you gain more experience and comfort with the lifestyle, you'll discover how easy it is to make a life for yourself anywhere you go. Going rural can add a degree of difficulty to going nomad, however — a higher language barrier, more difficulty finding the things you need or want, slower or less reliable internet — so I'd strongly recommend your first stop be a city of some size.

A few places are in the 'consider carefully' category — if the previous places each got a green light, these places would get a yellow light:

- **China** — although it has a cheaper cost of living and good internet, the level of control the country exercises over many matters of life, along with the so-called 'Great Firewall' (the country's strict control and censorship of the internet) can make interacting with people outside China much more difficult than necessary. Even something as simple as a local phone number and signing up for local services isn't really set up for foreigners. Consider Taiwan or Hong Kong instead, which have more freedom, but are more expensive.
- **India** — while it presents itself as a wonderful and cheap tourist destination (especially for all the budding yoga teachers out there), the slow internet, the costly visas, the bureaucracy, the pollution, and the chaotic nature of some cities can make settling in difficult. Consider Thailand or Malaysia instead.
- **The Philippines, Cambodia, and Laos** — these are some of the cheapest countries to call home, but the internet is slow and basic infrastructure is often lacking. Consider Thailand or Vietnam for nearby and affordable options, or Romania as another relatively cheap option.

While the world has many wonderful places to visit — these places get a red light for digital nomads:
- **Japan and South Korea** — there's plenty of culture in these first-world countries, but both are expensive to live in and neither has much in the way of English-language services. Expats often make it work, but even people who have lived there for years can run into issues.
- **The USA** — for non-Americans, getting a visa to get into and legally work in the USA can be an expensive, bureaucratic nightmare. While public transportation is available in the country's large cities, they're also some of the most expensive places to live in the country. If you have the financial means to live here and need to network in-person, it might be worthwhile.
- **Saudi Arabia, Egypt, Iran, or Yemen** — to be sure, it's not very likely these countries were actually on your list. The conservative Muslim countries are not exactly parts of the world that are open-minded towards trying new things, and there's not much support or community in these locations anyway.
- **Mongolia or much of sub-Saharan Africa** — these countries may offer plenty of gorgeous views to its tourists, but you're not a tourist. A solid connection to the internet is crucial to this lifestyle, and that can be difficult or costly to find in these countries.

What's this 'Schengen Zone' you've mentioned? It's a large region of western and central European countries that have no passport checks or border controls at their respective borders. You'll cross an international border without even needing to slow down. This agreement was signed in Schengen, Luxembourg in June 1985, and today includes 26 countries (with additional European countries legally obligated to join in the future). If you're a citizen or resident in one Schengen Zone country, you have the freedom to live and work in any other Schengen Zone country. If you're from the USA, Canada, or another non-Schengen-Zone country, you can only stay as a tourist in the Schengen Zone for up to 90 days at a time. You then have to go elsewhere for 90 days before you can return.

If you have a New Zealand passport, you have a pretty sweet deal. New Zealand has individual bilateral visa waiver agreements with the following Schengen signatories: Austria, Belgium, Czech Republic, Denmark, Finland, France, Germany, Greece, Iceland, Italy, Luxembourg, Netherlands, Norway, Portugal, Spain, Sweden, and Switzerland. Those agreements override the conditions of the Schengen Zone, so you'll get three months visa-free in *each country*, not just the zone as a whole. See wikipedia.org/wiki/Visa_requirements_for_New_Zealand_citizens for details. It would be prudent to have some proof of your travel from one country to the next in case you're ever asked about it.

With this as a primer, it's time to start brainstorming which parts of the world most interest you.

Worksheet #3: brainstorming

Date: _____

Find this at becomingadigitalnomad.com/worksheet3. Print a copy and complete offline, or complete online, then print or save.

List 5-10 countries or cities you think you'd like and/or that you've heard good things about. Don't worry about how expensive they are, how far away they are, the weather, or anything else. We'll narrow it down later on, but for right now, just write down any countries or cities you get good vibes about:

#1: I think _____ would be great to see because _____ .

#2: I think _____ would be great to see because _____ .

#3: I think _____ would be great to see because _____ .

#4: I think _____ would be great to see because _____ .

#5: I think _____ would be great to see because _____ .

#6: I think _____ would be great to see because _____.

#7: I think _____ would be great to see because _____.

#8: I think _____ would be great to see because _____.

#9: I think _____ would be great to see because _____.

#10: I think _____ would be great to see because _____.

Resources for researching your potential destinations

Now that you have an idea of your priorities and what places interest you, it's time to see where the two intersect.

There's plenty of research to do, so start by researching the cities and countries from your brainstorming on these sites:
- nomadlist.com — a site that offers lots of ratings in different countries around the world. Use their many filters to do a deep dive into what's most important to you, but don't eliminate places based solely on those filters (qualifications for those filters are often based on other users, and won't be uniformly or fairly given)

- numbeo.com — the "world's largest database of user contributed data about cities and countries worldwide," complete with millions of data points. It's a good place to gather the numbers to see which place is cheaper.
- teleport.org — start with their two-step process by choosing important tags, then enter a few details about where you are currently. Wade into the high-level overview of cities to consider, then get knee-deep in details and stats if you want.
- wikitravel.org — written by travelers for travelers, the tone can be a bit more casual (or snarky) than the more professionally written Wikipedia. Watch out for outdated material, and don't hesitate to edit it to make it more accurate!
- wherecani.live — started by a couple of Brits, the site takes you through a few steps of questions to determine which countries might be open to you, based on where you're from, where your grandparents (or great-grandparents) are from, investment or annual income potential, and so on. The site shows you specific countries and visa types for free, and also produces a full report for a nominal fee with more details.

Feel free to eliminate locations that no longer work for you, or add in some new options — this is *your* dream, after all!

What are some things to look for?
These will be based on your personal preferences — some folks love the heat, the big city, and so on. Try to remember to look at the country level, not the city level.

- The internet speed — the faster, the better.
- How the place is being talked about online — beyond the sites mentioned, search for terms like 'digital nomad [name of city]' 'digital nomad blog [name of city]' or 'expats in [name of city]'. Take what you see with a grain of salt, especially where affiliate links are concerned.
- The general budget — does the city have offerings in your budget?

- The climate, the greenspace, and the local mindset regarding foreigners.

Find your 'why'

As talked about earlier, people become digital nomads for plenty of reasons. These reasons fall into one of two categories: things that 'push' you away (or out of) your home country, and things that 'pull' you towards another country.

Some 'push' examples:
- Wanting to escape or get away
- Wanting to feel safe or safer
- Wanting to feel free (if you don't currently)
- Wanting to get out of your comfort zone
- Wanting to go somewhere you can afford to live

Some 'pull' examples:
- Wanting to try the food or culture in another country
- Wanting to see some of the sights in a country
- Wanting to explore the culture somewhere else

Know the political climate

As nomads, we're not in a position to take sides in politics, or even claim to know what's really going on in a place where we're essentially a tourist. It's up the locals to decide how best to handle their nation's issues, and as a guest, it's not our place to get involved. If we go to another country, we have to deal with the political climate as it exists — but *only to the point that it affects us*. Basic political nonsense probably won't affect you. A growing sense of xenophobia probably will affect you.

I mention it here because a story on cable news or a sensationalized newspaper article can give someone that cares about you a reason to try and talk you out of your plans. Their entire knowledge of the place may come from that one article, which almost certainly lacks the context needed to understand what's really going on there. I can't tell you how to change someone's mind, but you can typically rest their mind by reminding them you've done your research, that you're taking all the usual precautions, that you're an adult, and so on.

The political climate can be described as 'welcoming', 'hostile', 'friendly', 'xenophobic', 'tense', or in many other ways. Protests, riots, elections, money matters, sports matches, and many other things can shape the political climate. How much these affect your life will vary dramatically based on the country (and even the city) and where you are in it.

How do I research the political climate of where I'm going? It's worth paying attention to the local news websites and Facebook groups *in that country* to hear how much (if anything) the political climate is affecting people's lives. Sources like the BBC, the New York Times, the Associated Press, Reuters, and Bloomberg will generally have some of the most accurate reporting, though their coverage may still be flavored by their publication's biases. If there have been any troubling trends that affect travelers, Lonely Planet or Wikitravel are likely to have something on the issues on the summary / intro webpage of that country.

Just as you may not agree with your own country's politicians, locals may feel the same way about theirs. Much like in your home country, things like politics, religion, and sex almost never need to come up as a matter of casual conversation. Whatever your own political views may be, I urge you to keep them to yourself while traveling.

OK, that's one heavy subject over and done with. Let's move on.

Now that you've done some research, take a minute to write your finalists on the following worksheet.

Worksheet #4: the finalists — my most likely destinations

Date: _____

Find this at becomingadigitalnomad.com/worksheet4. Print a copy and complete offline, or complete online, print or save.

Start by copying your cities and / or countries from worksheet #3, then complete the rest.

City / country	Finalist or eliminated?	Why?

Of these finalists…

My favorite is _____ ,

because _____ .

My second favorite is _____ ,

because _____ .

My third favorite is _____ ,

because _____ .

Wrapping it all up

Of the eight steps in this book, I think this first step is the most exciting step. I'm sure the dozens of questions in the first worksheet probably felt like a lot, but that level of introspection and reflection puts you on the right track from the start. Becoming a digital nomad means following *your* dreams, not just going with the flow — and you're well on your way.

Step 2: Clarify your desires and acknowledge limitations

"You don't have to see the whole staircase to take the first step." — Martin Luther King, Jr.

OK, so we've taken a nice introspective look at ourselves and our desires, and it's time to home in on those dreams and begin thinking about the best ways to fulfill them. At the same time, we've also got to talk about the things that can stand in our way. They can be money, time, the people that are close to us, physical limitations, and other issues. Whatever they may be, we need to acknowledge them before we can address them and ultimately take care of them.

Let's jump right into this topic with the next worksheet about clarifying desires.

Worksheet #5: Clarifying desires

Date: _____

Find this at becomingadigitalnomad.com/worksheet5. Print a copy and complete offline, or complete online, then print or save.

Of the many things you'd *like* to do as a digital nomad, what are a few of your strongest or most urgent desires? (This isn't about any one specific facet of your life. Write what's truly important to you — there are no 'right' or 'wrong' answers here.)

#1: I **most want to** _____

because _____ .

#2: I **also want to** _____

because _____ .

#3: I'd **really like to** _____

because _____ .

Are any of these desires best done — or only possible to do — in specific countries, cities, or types of locations?

#1 is possible **in / at / on** _____ .

#2 is possible **in / at / on** _____ .

#3 is possible **in / at / on** _____ .

While we haven't yet talked much about work, will any of your jobs or gigs need to be done in a certain type of place?

In order to _____ ,

I'll need to be in / at / near _____ .

What do you want to be near?

I'd like to be near _____

because _____ .

Nomads vs. expats

As you're thinking about and researching the digital nomad lifestyle, I want to differentiate the *nomad* lifestyle and the *expat* lifestyle in your mind. You'll hear or see both terms as you're researching or planning… but what's the difference?

- A nomad will typically live somewhere for shorter periods of time (usually up to three months), while an expat will live somewhere for longer periods of time (from three months up to a year, or even longer)
- A nomad will typically stay in a furnished apartment or room, while an expat may choose to furnish a place themselves. The expat is staying in the same place for longer, so expats may also customize their home more.
- A nomad will typically enter a country on a tourist visa, but may also arrange for an educational, business, or other type of visa. An expat will typically enter a country with a work, business, or educational visa, since they intend to stay for a longer period of time.
- Expats may have to meet more rigid expectations, such as when they should arrive, or when they can travel. This is

usually because of their job, which is often the reason they're moving there. Nomads generally have fewer expectations to meet.
- Expats are more likely to have a traditional job, and they become more connected to locals through their work. Nomads are less likely to have a traditional job, and must work harder and be more proactive to connect with locals.

So it's clear, both the nomad lifestyle and the expat lifestyle can be thoroughly enjoyed. Becoming an *expat* is outside the scope of this book, but a lot of principles are the same whether you plan to become an expat or a nomad. The time periods are just different.

Getting ready — what to do next

So you've pinpointed two or three destinations and you've clarified your desires. It's not too early to start to think about how you might live in that location, as well as to start dealing with your stuff. Obviously, the sooner you can start to work out how much all of this is going to cost you — and where the money's going to come from — the better. This next part has the resources and information that will help you work through these three important issues.

Finding a new place to live

Once you've pinpointed a location, how do you find out where to live? These days, there are four worthy options, and an honorable mention:

1. Live with a host family.
2. Try life in a co-living space.
3. Live on your own in your own place.
4. Work as a housesitter and live in other people's houses while caring for their houses, pets, plants, etc.

5. **Honorable mention:** Nanouk van Gennip mentions "travel in an RV" — a great option if you're willing to drive your way around the country and aren't planning to cross oceans. This isn't as great for crossing a ton of borders, but can still be an option.

Let's take a longer look at these options.

Living with a host family

The biggest benefit to living with a host family (AKA doing a homestay) is **embracing the local culture**. You'll get a first-hand look into how locals live, since you'll be living alongside them, but you'll need to be prepared to follow their rules. A homestay is typically one of the cheapest options, especially if you live, eat, and party as the locals do. Note that your host might regard the arrangement as a cultural exchange and take special care to introduce you to their way of life, or they might simply consider it a business transaction and leave you on your own to do as you please. Ask questions and read profiles carefully to see how hands-on (or off) the hosts will be.

Some options to find homestays:
- borderless-house.com — 'multicultural share houses' are 50% locals, 50% foreigners. Available in Japan, Korea, and Taiwan. Be aware there is an age limit.
- chinet.org — this non-profit offers 11 different cultural exchange programs for studying, working, or traveling abroad. These are short-term programs and are primarily aimed at students.
- homestay.com — "offers guests the chance to live like — and with — a local with more than 50,000 homestays in over 160 countries and to discover a truly authentic travel experience." The website has a similar look and feel to Airbnb.
- homestayfinder.com — "helping host families and international students to find each other." Charges a

monthly fee. A rather old-looking site, and you'll need to send a message to hosts to confirm availability.
- homestayin.com — free to join. Pay a 10 or 15% deposit online to confirm your homestay, then pay the rest of the fee to your host directly. Primarily in larger cities in the US, Europe, and Oceania.
- homestayweb.com — newly re-designed as of October 2018. Free to register, but charges a monthly fee to send messages to any host on the platform.
- lingoo.com — "book unique language exchange holidays and homestays or stay with a teacher". Supposedly the "world's biggest language exchange and homestay club", the site offers paid or exchange stays. Charges an annual fee.

Beyond these are other regional options best found by searching for 'homestay [city / country]'.

Co-living space

Life in a co-living space means you're **almost always around other nomads**. Some places will plan trips together, have you eating together, and/or take you out for parties together. See roam.co, 20mission.com, cowoli.com, outsite.co, or just Google 'co-living [city]' to find programs around the world.

The business model here is to offer a number of apartments / houses / communal places specifically for digital nomads, *without* making travel a part of the deal. The biggest issue here is that living with a group of nomads can easily become a 'bubble' that separates you from the location and the locals. It's usually so much easier to socialize with the people you live with rather than exploring on your own. Also, your share of a co-living space can cost more than a similarly-sized Airbnb or other furnished apartment. If considering this option, do some price checks before committing.

(A ***co-working*** space, by comparison is *not* a place to live. Head to a co-working space to get a desk and a fast internet connection, and network with other entrepreneurs.)

I do not recommend traveling with a co-living ***group***, which is a different concept from the co-living ***spaces*** mentioned above. These companies will bring the *group* together, then move the group to different *locations* for certain lengths of time. Once you've joined the group, you travel where and when they do. This is basically the business model behind Remote Year, Hacker Paradise, Embark Together, Nomad House, and other similar programs. These businesses aren't interested in teaching you how to live independently or giving you many choices, and you'll have to conform to their mindsets and expectations as well. If you don't mind paying a premium for having everything set up and magically arranged, ***and*** you're OK with the places the program takes you and the people you'll be with, it might be worth considering. Those are some big 'ifs', though.

Get your own place

For most nomads, getting your own place offers the **best balance of freedom and flexibility**. When my wife and I first started living as nomads, we would typically book a hotel for a week or so while looking for apartments on local websites, Facebook groups, and so on. We wanted to see a place for ourselves before committing or signing any sort of contract (and *definitely* before putting any sort of money down on a place, so as to avoid scams).

This worked, though we didn't always find a lot of viable choices that quickly. Most tourist visas are for three months, which ends up being an awkward length of time for a traditional lease. If you'll be arriving on a longer-term visa, a six-month or one-year traditional lease is a better option.

While some platforms will also rent you a room, renting out the entire apartment really lets you be on your own. I definitely recommend this option if you're traveling with kids or a life partner. Some well-known platforms (in alphabetical order):

- agoda.com — millions of listings, but you can only get a place for a maximum of 30 days. Often price-competitive, but research listings and reviews.
- airbnb.com — you've probably heard of them. Easily the largest platform of its kind, with listings for all budgets and locations. Ubiquitous monthly discounts.
- ebab.com — "Your way to stay 100% gay." Stands for 'enjoy bed and breakfast'.
- flipkey.com — "FlipKey is a vacation rental marketplace with more than 300,000 rentals around the world." Part of Tripadvisor's network of businesses.
- homeaway.com — claiming two million homes in more than 190 countries, the site has lots of filters hidden under the 'More Filters' button.
- innclusive.com — after having issues getting an Airbnb because of the color of his skin, Rohan Gilkes built a platform of his own. Hosts are required to be — wait for it — inclusive, and a solid boost of publicity went a long way to building a network of diverse hosts and offerings around the world.
- misterbandb.com — 135 countries and 200,000 listings specifically for gay men.
- spotahome.com — "the easiest way to find and book your mid to long-term housing." Houses are supposedly checked / validated by their Homecheckers, but despite their promises of having their professionals visit every property, some aren't / haven't. Often requires large deposits like traditional apartments. *Currently only offers places in a couple dozen major European cities.*
- tripping.com — a metasearch engine that combines listings from HomeAway, VRBO, TripAdvisor, Booking.com, and so on.

- VRBO.com — Vacation Rental By Owner, in case you were curious. Claims over two million house rentals available worldwide, but no monthly discounts.
- wimbify.com — "Wimbify is a PeerToPeer platform of Social Travel Sharing, dedicated to the LGBT community". The website is essentially just a promotional plug for the apps.
- wimdu.com — "Europe's biggest portal for city and holiday apartments." Some monthly discounts, but they vary.

Find the perfect place

We started using Airbnb in 2015 and with the exception of a handful of nights in hotels, we haven't looked back. Airbnb is a great fit for digital nomads for plenty of reasons:
- Apartments are always furnished.
- Plenty of budget and size options, from the whole apartment to just your own room in a shared house.
- It's the biggest platform of its kind for finding places to stay around the world, with listings in over 190 countries.
- If anything goes wrong, the platform can help resolve issues.
- The host is often a wealth of knowledge about their city / country.

To be sure, Airbnb is not without its fair share of controversy, and there are bad apples on all sides of the equation. Detractors of Airbnb will point out that housing used for Airbnb's equals more housing not lived in by locals, which drives down supply and drives up demand. Supporters of Airbnb point to the income generated for locals, the wide variety of places to stay, and so on. Some cities and countries have passed laws limiting or prohibiting Airbnb listings as a result, though enforcement of those laws varies greatly. There's no shortage of challenges surrounding Airbnb, but it remains one of the best options for digital nomads at this time.

Whether you use Airbnb or another site, here's how to find a great place:

- Start by knowing what's important to you (and anyone else you're traveling with). Lots of open space? Fast wi-fi? Big kitchen? A big bed?
- Choose what part of the city you want to be in. Do you want to be in the heart of downtown, by the biggest park in the city, or in the suburbs? You might also choose to start city-wide, then use the scale to show what's available on your budget.
- Click on 5-10 listings. Hold down 'Ctrl' or 'Command' in your keyboard while clicking so they open in new tabs in your browser.
- Look at the pictures. We'll get to the text in a moment — for now, just look at the pictures. Try to get a sense of the layout and how the place looks. Does it have the things you're looking for? (Since my wife and I both work at home, we're looking for two desks and chairs, doors that close the rooms off, and a coffee maker for me.)
- *Always* click 'read more about the space', then start reading the descriptions. Overlook the fluff (such as 'only 5 minutes to downtown!'), but pay attention to what it says about things that are nearby (like bus or metro stops, grocery stores, etc.)
- Confirm what you're renting: the entire apartment, a private room, or a shared room. It can be easily overlooked.
- If staying for longer than a month, confirm you're receiving a monthly discount from the usual nightly rate. Hosts can set the percentage of the monthly discount amounts themselves, so the bigger the better. Check the cleaning fees and deposit necessary while you're here. Next, read the reviews and responses from the last year or so.
- If all the details look good, keep the tab open. Narrow it down to the best 2 or 3, then pick one. Bonus points if it's an Instant Book so you get a reservation made as soon as you pay. **If it's a 'Request to Book' listing, only request to book one place at a time.**

Airbnb will collect some money in anticipation of a 'yes', and the host will have 24 hours to respond to your request. In case they decline, make a note of the other finalists and request one of them next.

House-sitting

House-sitting can be a win-win for you and the homeowner. You get to stay in a place that's free, greatly reduced in rent, or perhaps even paying you to stay there. The homeowner, meanwhile saves money getting the care they need for their house, pets, plants, and so on. (If you dislike caring for someone else's animals or are unable to do so for whatever reason, it may restrict the number of house-sitting gigs open to you.)

The biggest downside to house-sitting: you might feel like you're stuck in a location for longer than you want, and it might be difficult to travel around the area. Also, being flexible and going where the houses are is a shift from the 'go where you want' mindset.

Here's how house-sitting typically works:
- Sign up to be a housesitter on a platform. Bear in mind these are just some of the larger sites, and there are others more focused on specific parts of the world.
    - caretaker.org
    - housecarers.com (note this is *not* 'house careers')
    - housesitmatch.com
    - housesitter.com
    - luxuryhousesitting.com
    - mindmyhouse.com
    - nomador.com
    - trustedhousesitters.com
- If possible, do a house-sit for friends, family, etc. to get a reference or two, but also get a sense of what to expect. Ask your landlord or boss for a reference, too — the more the merrier!

- Fill out your profile on the website(s) you choose. Bear in mind that homeowners are essentially awarding you (potentially) thousands of dollars worth of accommodation, and their decision is often based on how your profile looks. Have a look at the popular or highest-rated profiles on the site to see how they make use of their profile's space, then aim to do better. Don't forget to check your spelling and grammar!
- Get good, in-focus photos of you with your pets (if you have them). The pictures don't have to be professionally taken, but they should make you look like a pleasant human being.
- Reach out and send a message whenever a good fit comes along. This is a numbers game, so send messages to fill your schedule.
- Emphasize your experience, your love of pets, your ability to care for plants, your self-sufficiency, your willingness or ability to follow directions, and so on.
- Browse the site frequently, and stay on top of what homeowners are saying in their reviews of other housesitters. This feedback can guide what you say in your profile, your messages to them, etc.
- Ask questions to ensure you know what's allowed or not allowed. Read the profile carefully first, though, to see if your questions have already been answered. Among many questions that might be relevant:
    - How are utility bills handled? The garbage / recycling?
    - Is the house listed for sale (meaning real estate agents might be showing the place, so part of your job might mean keeping it presentable)?
    - If there are pets, what are their routines? Their character / personality?
    - Is a security deposit required?
    - Are guests allowed?
    - Can you bring your own pets?
    - If there's a vehicle, are you allowed to use it? How is insurance for this handled?
    - If any money is being exchanged, how is that being handled (through the site, Paypal, etc.)?

- Know the weather and climate for the area. The house-sitting job you accepted for January to March may involve lots of snow shoveling, for example. A Northern Hemisphere garden from April to June may require more work if tending to the garden is part of the job.

Once you get a 'yes', follow the directions provided by your host to ensure a good connection / check-in. A few rules are paramount:

- Take care of the place. You literally have one job, as far as the homeowner is concerned, and screwing this up can make future house-sitting jobs a lot harder to get. This usually goes beyond 'take care of it like you would your own', it's more like 'take care of it like you'll be paying dearly for it if something breaks'.
- Leave the place better / cleaner than you found it.
- Keep the owner's guidelines in mind, and ask them for clarification as needed.
- If something happens, honesty remains the best policy.

Once you've left, don't forget to give (and elicit) a review. Those references can make future house-sitting jobs even easier to get.

One excellent resource put together by fellow nomads is an e-book at hecktictravels.com/housesitting. They go over a lot of the basic steps to a house-sit in greater detail, but also share their own stories of house-sitting and how much it's saved them over the years.

RV's — a home on wheels

Traveling in a Recreational Vehicle (RV) might be the very definition of a nomadic lifestyle. There's a more obvious up-front investment in the vehicle, of course, and you're going to be limited on how much traveling you might do from one continent to the next. Depending on the vehicle's registration and the countries in question, the red tape for entering another country might be substantial. Still, the housing expense is already paid for, it's easy to pack up and go anytime you want, and it can be a great family experience. If you plan to spend more time in nature or rural areas instead of bigger cities, or if you're considering traveling with pets, this is a great option. (A good search engine for pet-friendly hotels, when you're ready for a break from the RV: tripswithpets.com.)

Bear in mind that while your 'housing' may be covered, you'll need to park somewhere for the night. This might be at full-on RV resorts, campsites with RV parking lots, a park that allows overnight parking, or perhaps a store's parking lot. These costs can add up, though it'll still be cheaper than an apartment! (Note that 'boondocking', or staying for free wherever you can park overnight without running afoul of the law, is a thing. This may limit your access to hook-ups and be subject to other limits, but plenty of people are doing it.)

More than a few digital nomads write about their RV adventures:
- carolynsrvlife.com — give you one guess who rocks a 29-foot 1993 Class C RV. Carolyn's story is of a single woman traveling via RV since April 2016.
- rvwanderlust.com — Eric, Brittany, and their son Caspian have traveled in an RV called Meriwether since 2014.
- smallrvlifestyle.com — Viktoria is originally from Hungary and travels in a 'Micro Class C' RV, which she says "feels like a small apartment."
- technomadia.com — Cherie and Chris hit the road in 2006 in their vintage bus, 'Zephyr', and have a book dedicated to finding the internet while RVing at rvmobileinternet.com/book.
- westfaliadigitalnomads.com — Armando and Mel live in a van called Mork which has taken them across Europe and North America.

Other options

Beyond apartment booking sites and house-sitting sites, your best bet might well be **Facebook groups.** There's a Facebook group for almost anything these days, though they'll vary greatly by quality and size. They run the gamut, and might aim to provide information, social commentary, buy / sell / trade listings, apartments / rooms for rent, and so on. The number of members shouldn't be considered an accurate count, however, since people rarely remember to leave these groups when they've left the area. Focus on the frequency of posts and their general tone instead.

Find a group by typing the city or country name and 'nomads' into Facebook's search bar, then hit Enter. Click 'Groups' at the top of Facebook's search results page, then start joining whichever groups sound interesting. Once you're in, click the 'More' button just below the big picture and click 'Pin to Favorites'. This makes it easier to find the group later on, and makes a nice little reminder on the left sidebar to check-in with what's new.

If you're American, **Craigslist** (craigslist.org) is a well-known site for finding almost anything. While it's a decent resource in the US, the scams and spam can overwhelm the legitimate offerings in other countries. In smaller countries, the only craigslist board will be for the capital city or perhaps another major city, and some countries aren't even on the site. It might be worth checking if you're going to a larger city, but otherwise I'd steer clear.

Most countries have a Craigslist-type of site for buying and selling almost anything. They might be worth finding and perusing, but bear in mind they're rarely optimized for non-local languages (meaning Google Translate is your friend if you decide to try them).

The traditional methods for finding apartments certainly haven't gone anywhere. Agencies and people that put out 'for lease' signs on their property are still alive and kicking in many parts of the world. Most of them, however, are geared towards a more 'traditional' lease of the one year or longer variety, and language barriers can also be an issue. If you'll be in a specific place for that long, then by all means feel free to work with traditional apartment rental agencies.

Home vs. Base

As you're reading and researching things, you'll come across some nomads who refer to their 'base' or their 'homebase' instead of their 'home'. To some, home is the city they grew up, where their parents live, or somewhere else in their home country. They might use the word 'base' or 'homebase' to differentiate between where they're staying and where they call home. Other people prefer 'base' if they have more than one place they switch between.

Personally, 'home' is wherever I happen to be sleeping. It's where the wi-fi connects automatically. It's not a place I imbue lots of emotional attachments to. This is different for everyone, naturally.

Ways to deal with your stuff

Beyond where to live, one major limitation people have when embracing the digital nomad lifestyle is *stuff*. Everyone seems to have far more stuff than they know what to do with, and you can't take it all with you. To make matters worse, you've probably read some articles about how some digital nomads make it sound easy to live out of a single carry-on bag or a large backpack. **Enough of that — how much stuff you choose to take is up to you.** We'll get to a packing list later on, but understand the packing list will look pretty similar no matter how long you'll be gone.

Before I left for Korea, I sold my car, left a lot of furniture with my then-roommate, and took four huge bags of clothes to the local second-hand store. I asked my parents to store some personal effects from my younger years, I didn't have a lot of decorations to get rid of, but just living in a place for a while means you collect stuff without thinking about it. You can call it inertia, deadweight, or just *stuff* — whatever you call it, it can't all go with you.

Whether it's methodically or haphazardly done, *minimalism* is the name of the game. **Simply put, the goal isn't to figure out what you can live *with*, it's to figure out *what you can't live without*.** Minimalism is not about being cheap or getting down to a bare minimum or spartan type of lifestyle. Just like you're creating your new life, you're also creating your own new rules of what you need in this new version of reality. What you own no longer tells people who you are.

Tyler Durden said it best in the movie Fight Club: "The things you own end up owning you." Whether they tie you down or keep you from being as mobile as you like, stuff can accumulate and surround you to a point where it really does own you. That's the bad news — the good news? You *need* a lot less than you *have* — narrowing it down and getting what you need into your suitcase(s) and/or backpack.

Personally, there are three elements I take into consideration: **weight, replaceability, and cost.** Things that are lighter (or less bulky), harder to replace, and more expensive should be much more likely to go with you. Things that are heavier or bulkier, easier to replace, and less expensive should be less likely to be packed, since it might be better to buy them once you arrive. Things that are in the middle have to be evaluated on a case-by-case basis, along with how often you'll use it. In general, things that can be rented the few times you want to use them (think roller skates, skis, sports equipment, gym equipment, etc.) are best left behind. These also tend to be heavy and bulky — even more reason to rent wherever you go!

Another great acid test (with credit to Fumio Sasaki in the book *Goodbye, Things*): "If I were to somehow lose this, would I want to buy it again at full price?"

This list can look rather short, and you might be wondering 'what about the rest of my stuff?' There are basically five options, and I've put them in the order to do them:

- throw it away
- sell it
- give it away
- store it
- take it with you

While it's just meant as a guide, the recommended packing list can be found in step 5 ('What to Pack').

Cleaning house — throw it away

Throw away anything best described as 'old', 'expired', 'with holes', 'junk', 'worn', or 'worn out' — anything that wouldn't be accepted at your local charity / second-hand store. Just throw it out. Your antiques are safe since they're 'antique' or 'vintage' — right now, I'm talking about that 10-year-old pair of shoes in the back of your closet you haven't worn in years. If you haven't worn it or used it in a year, it's time for it to go. Anything you promised to get around to 'someday'? Yeah, that's probably gotta go.

One thing that'll be worth considering: how did you accumulate all this stuff in the first place? Hobbies, relationships, a desire to look trendy, shopping at garage sales, or just general inertia? Without changing your habits, you'll have to be on guard to avoid repeating the same mistakes.

Make some money for your journey: sell it

What should you sell, specifically? As a start, clothes, furniture, appliances, electronics, books, antiques, collectibles, and any other stuff not coming with you. Price to sell and move, and don't worry about what the price was originally. Remember that the current value of something is nowhere near the original price you paid, and the prices you see on Craigslist or other buy-and-sell sites prove that. Aim to sell fewer big-ticket items over more smaller-ticket items, if only to avoid having to meet and deal with more people. Not worth the hassle to do it yourself? Use a pickup service that creates the ads, meets with buyers, then sends you your cut.

As you're letting go of things, try to let go of the notion that you need to get your money's worth out of it. For one, you've already spent the money, which makes it a 'sunk cost' in economist-speak. For another, as you're looking around, you'll probably realize this describes a fair bit of your stuff!

Be generous — give it away

Anything you didn't (or couldn't) sell? There's bound to be plenty of worthy causes, charity shops, and second-hand stores around — and some might even be able to arrange a pick-up. Remember to save the tax receipts if donating. Giving stuff away should also mean giving things to friends and family — especially things of sentimental value. Be sure to let them know if this is a permanent 'gift', or if they're just storing things for you until you get back. After years of ownership, it may have found a place in their home and they might not want to let it go!

The option of last resort — store it

We're left with stuff we'd rather not throw away, haven't sold, and don't want to give away — but can't or shouldn't take with us. Do everything you can to store stuff with friends or family if necessary, and avoid storage units that have monthly fees.

What if I'm just testing things out? If you're just testing the lifestyle out, storage is more acceptable. The catch? If you decide to stick with the nomadic lifestyle, you'll have to deal with all that stuff at some point. It can be really tempting to put everything in storage and put off actually dealing with it, but all the while you're paying a monthly fee just to keep your stuff safe. Worse, you might forget to pay the bills and have your stuff auctioned off as a result. After a couple of years, you may have spent as much on storage fees as the stuff is worth. The more stuff you leave behind, the harder it can be to really leave the old life behind.

Take it with you

Even after you've reached this stage, you may be facing an uncomfortable truth: it doesn't all fit. Time to look at what's left — do you really need to take 20 t-shirts? Are you about to take something bulky that's cheap and easy to repurchase? Again, there's more advice and the recommended packing list in step 5 ('What to Pack').

Two cautions here:
- Along the way, you'll have organized your stuff better than it's been organized in awhile. Organizing is not minimizing, however — the goal is not to make stuff fit in a smaller space or to pack it more efficiently. **The goal is to have less stuff.**
- Just because it *fits* doesn't mean it *weighs* the correct amount. You'll be lugging this around for awhile, up stairs, down crappy sidewalks, and around town.

Airlines are notorious for being sticklers about weight and won't hesitate to overcharge for extra weight.

Nostalgia and memories

One big challenge for many future nomads is to let go of nostalgia. We all have things we hang onto because they bring back great memories, but we've got to get stuff in this category down to a minimum. Ideally, nostalgia won't weigh anything extra or take up any extra space. The longer you've lived in one place, the harder it can be to let go of what you've accumulated. Take heart — like anything else in life, it gets easier the more often you do it.

Wait, how do we make nostalgia weigh nothing? Digitize and upload to a free cloud-based service wherever possible. Some examples:

- Upload pictures to photos.google.com — download a free program to upload unlimited numbers of photos (note they will be downscaled from their original size). You might also consider paid plans on Flickr Pro, Amazon Photos, or Shoebox.
- Upload videos to youtube.com or vimeo.com (you can set them to 'unlisted' so only people with the link can access them)
- Upload audio to soundcloud.com or anchor.fm.
- Upload files to Dropbox.com, box.com, Google Drive, or Microsoft OneDrive.

Give the original photos, videotapes, memory cards, and other media to your family members or a trusted friend to hold onto.

The minimalist philosophy — and its rewards

By their very nature, digital nomads are minimalists — people who know what's essential to their lives. There's a trade-off to be made — your freedom to travel means that floor-to-ceiling shelf of books can't go with you. There's an excellent book entitled *Goodbye, Things: The New Japanese Minimalism* by Fumio Sasaki that gets into the philosophy of minimalism. While I don't subscribe to the extreme type of minimalism found in this book, there's a balance to be found here.

Personally, my goal is to be able to carry, push, or pull everything you own at the same time in one trip.

There's a correlation between the number of things you have to deal with in your everyday life and the number of distractions from what matters in your life. Money doesn't buy happiness, and minimalism is not a competition. To the nomads who can get their entire lives into a backpack, bravo — but again, it's not a competition. Just get it in the bag and get going.

Becoming a digital nomad puts the hardest parts of the transition into the first couple of steps. We can easily come up with lots of creative reasons for why we shouldn't get rid of something — *I was saving this for a project! So* that's *where it went! I never finished that book!* — but they need to be ignored.

You said something about rewards? Beyond the fact that minimalism makes your traveling life easier, it will soon begin to feel like you're not lacking or missing anything. The stuff you have will do everything you need it to. Also, it makes buying stuff (when you need to) a lot easier — to mesh with the rest of your lifestyle, it needs to be a quality thing, lightweight, easy to clean / use, and possibly even have more than one use. Buying something new usually means replacing something old or worn out to avoid adding more stuff to your bag.

One final time: it's not a competition. Avoid boasting that you 'only' need a backpack or judging others that have more (or less) than you.

Budgeting: the 64,000,000-yen question

As you start to put the puzzle pieces together, one essential question focuses on your budget. **What is your budget for spending per month? What savings do you have?** We'll get to how digital nomads make money in the next step, but for now, start by assuming you'll make *zero* money while traveling. That's basically the worst-case scenario, and for most people it's unlikely to happen. It can happen, though, and you should be aware of that possibility.

As a digital nomad, you probably won't be tied to one job or company, and as a result you can expect your income to change. It's the *expenses* I'd like to focus on in this next worksheet — compare your current budget to your projected nomad budget.

Worksheet #6: monthly expenses

Date: _____

Find this at becomingadigitalnomad.com/worksheet6. Print a copy and complete offline, or complete online, then print or save.

Fill in what you spent last month (or average the last 3 months) on these various items. Use worksheet #12 in step 7 to keep track of your actual expenses.

Expenses	Current amount	Projected amount	Notes / how to estimate
Housing			Use the cost stated on the co-living / Airbnb space.
Utilities (electricity, water, gas)			It's fairly rare to pay utilities as a short-term nomad. Assume zero unless it's been mentioned.
Credit card payments			Assume you're making the same payments.
School loans			Assume you're making the same payments.

Entertainment			Fair to start with the same amount; adjust up or down after first month.
Groceries			Budget about the same to start.
Eating out			Budget about the same to start.
Alcohol / parties			Fair to start with the same amount; adjust up or down after first month.
Household needs (cleaning supplies)			Budget about the same to start.
Clothes			Start with a small amount to replace what wears out.
Health / wellness (vitamins, gym membership, medications)			May be cheaper depending on where you're from and where you're going.
Travel / Health Insurance			Discussed in greater detail later in the book. Use a quote from one website as an estimate.

Transportation (car payment, car insurance, gas / petrol, public transportation)			Will almost certainly be cheaper.
Internet / phone			Will almost certainly be cheaper.
Costs of doing business:	—-	—-	Can vary based on the services used.
Your website(s) (web hosting, domain names, web developer)			
Virtual assistant or other service providers			
Software products / online / subscription services			
Other costs of doing business			
Other expense #1 (_____ _____)			
Other expense #2 (_____)			
Other expense #3 (_____)			

Other expense #4 ( )			
Other expense #5 ( )			
Total			

How do I estimate my budget in a country I've never been to? Where you're going will have the biggest impact on your budget, but your specific desires or interests will also have a large influence. Start with numbeo.com to get a ballpark sense, plug in quotes or estimates as you receive them, then ask nomads online to validate or clarify your research.

Wherever you go, know you can save money just like you can at home — eat out less, drink less alcohol, live in a cheaper place, and so on. It's not rocket science, you just choose your priorities.

Other possible limitations to consider

As you begin to prepare for this transition, think about the balance you want to make between work and play. You really need to have a plan for this, but at the same time, leave some time and space for whatever may happen.

Are there any physical, mental, emotional, or spiritual issues you must work with?

Be honest with yourself here. What issues might you have to deal with? Would any part of starting this journey cause you anxiety, pain, an unusual level of stress, etc.?

If you use a wheelchair, research the city / country to see how accessible they are. Use Airbnb's search filters to find accessible properties that work for your specific needs. Check pantou.org (a worldwide accessible tourism directory), emerginghorizons.com (an excellent blog about accessible travel), or curbfreewithcorylee.com (a serious travel addict who just happens to use a wheelchair) for more information.

If you find it difficult to walk a lot, choosing a city with more public transportation (or easy-to-navigate taxis) might be important.

If you find it difficult to socialize, know how much (or how little) you choose to socialize is up to you. One does not need to attend every social event around, especially when there are plenty to go around. Some people gain energy from interacting with others, while others are left drained. If you really prefer your own company to that of others, think twice about booking any kind of shared accommodation, including a homestay. Having your own space to come back to after a day's exploration could well prove essential to your well-being.

If, on the other hand, you *want* to socialize, but aren't sure where to start, there are likely to be at least two friendly options around:

- **Couchsurfing** — it's not just a community for sleeping on someone's couch. It also lists hosts, upcoming visitors, people who are hanging out / want to hang out, and events. Start from couchsurfing.com/places or search the site for the city you're headed to. Once you're on the page for the city or country, scroll down to 'Events'. You can even publicly mention you're available to meet people.
- **Toastmasters** — one of the more supportive groups out there, both for people learning a language and for socializing with friendly people. Start from toastmasters.org/find-a-club and search for your location.

- **Internations** — is another platform dedicated to connecting expats and nomads around the world. Start at internations.org.

Beyond these three, seek out the local Facebook groups for expats, nomads, foreigners, or common interests and hobbies you enjoy. Most every city has locals looking to meet foreigners or practice their English.

If you think it will be difficult to be away from friends or family, think about the best ways to stay in touch with them. Skype is one well-known video-calling service, but your family might prefer Google Hangouts, Facebook Messenger, Apple's Facetime, or any number of VOIP (voice over internet protocol) calling apps like Whatsapp or Viber. (Alternatively, as Nanouk van Gennip says, "don't go that far. That's one of the reasons why we decided to stay in Europe. We're always one or two days driving from our family, or 2 hours by plane.")

If you're spiritual / religious and decide to leave your city / country (but still want to follow your religion), what's the best way to proceed? You might choose to find a new place of worship, or you might keep up with their services online. If applicable, use the website of your religion or denomination to find a local congregation, or ask local Facebook groups about which places of worship offer English-language services.

Soft skills — strengths, not limitations

Soft skills are basic attributes or skills that transfer with you from one job to the next, and can help in many different aspects of your life. Soft skills that will come in useful to a digital nomad include (in alphabetical order):

- Adaptability — adapting to the situation at hand, wherever you are.
- Budgeting / money management — this one's self-explanatory.

- Communication skills — communicating in a friendly and professional way.
- Curiosity — this one will really come in handy if you're going to live as a nomad! What's down that side street? What else does this coffeehouse make?
- Flexibility — things rarely go the way you planned.
- Language skills — being able to read, write, speak, and understand the local language.
- Optimism — this can be a 'glass-half-full' attitude, or just staying positive even when things aren't going well.
- Organization — getting and staying organized even as you move around the world.
- Problem solving — there are usually multiple options to solving a problem.
- Resourceful — making it work, finding another way, or using what you have to get something done.
- Self-discipline — staying focused on the thing you're working on and not getting distracted by lots of other things.
- Staying calm in stressful situations — this one's obvious enough, but it's also necessary since travel and life in unfamiliar places can be very stressful.
- Strong work ethic — treating work obligations and deadlines with seriousness and professionalism, even if it means missing out on fun stuff.
- Time management — knowing how to structure your time and getting work done before playing.

To be clear, nobody's perfect, and nobody will ever have every single soft skill. The goal here is to keep developing them, whether you're good at them or not.

Other considerations

Here are a few additional points to consider when you're deciding where you might want to go:

- **Are there any language barriers?** You're likely to find English speakers in most countries (based on the local education system and connectedness to the English-speaking world), but you'll still want to learn some of the local language.
- **Any specific dietary needs?** Some cities and countries are more friendly to vegetarians or vegans, as one example. If you're taking certain vitamins or supplements, you may want to stock up before leaving.
- **Do you like it hot or cold?** Some nomads plan their trips to 'follow the summer' and go from the northern hemisphere to the southern hemisphere, while others simply check for the best times to see each country and go from there.
- **Where will it be hot or cold (or warm)?** Think fourth dimensionally — if you already know when you'll be going, you can look up the climate of the area (including the average temperatures) at that time.
- **Will weather extremes be a real turn-off?** Places that get extremely hot or extremely cold aren't always as much fun, but they can make going swimming or skiing a lot more fun.

Who's coming with you? Traveling with others

More than a few nomads travel with their spouse, life partner, a traveling buddy, or perhaps their whole family. If you're single and have no kids, flying solo is typically the easiest scenario, since no one else's needs have to be accounted for. You need not *stay* solo, of course — there are plenty of ways to meet up with other nomads. If you're looking for something more than friendship, you might consider heading to nomadsoulmates.com to find other nomads in the area. Tinder is very much a thing in most cities around the world. I met my wife on OKCupid while teaching English in South Korea, and there are plenty of other apps or websites to meet other people as you travel.

If you're considering keeping a relationship going without taking that person with you, Candy Harrington has a warning to add: "I sometimes had a boyfriend who was not traveling with me and boy were those some rocky times. It's really hard to manage a relationship on the road, so if you're single or in a relationship and travel with your significant other, great. I'd really think twice about becoming a nomad and trying to carry on a long-distance relationship, though. It takes so much away from the travel experience if you aren't fully present, and if you have relationship issues a world away, you are always thinking about it."

Traveling with partner / spouse

(For the sake of argument, go ahead and lump in 'traveling with boyfriend / girlfriend / same-sex partner' here as well — if they're coming with you, the questions and thought processes are generally the same.)

Whether your traveling companion is a good friend, someone you're dating, a life partner, or a spouse, traveling with them can add a wrinkle of complexity. **Whoever they are, getting buy-in from them is critical — this lifestyle needs to be something you both want.**

Your needs and interests are not created equal, so start a conversation and start working together to plan your travels according to your needs. Some questions each of you need to answer:

- How connected do each of you need to be to the internet?
- Do you prefer faster or slower travel?
- What sort of budget are the two of you looking to live on?
- How much space does each of you need / want?
- Do either of you feel more connected to 'home' or family?

Once you're on the road, these are several necessary rules to making the lifestyle sustainable.

- **Rule #1: Don't be a dick**. I shouldn't have to say this, but there it is.
- **Give each other space**. When you're around someone all the time, it can feel like you have no privacy or space to yourself. To that end, we look for Airbnbs that have two rooms with doors that close. They can be bedrooms, living rooms, or offices. One person might set things up in the living room, while the other takes over the kitchen or the bedroom. The idea is that you can watch your own videos or listen to music, and otherwise call different spaces 'yours', 'mine', or 'ours'.
- **Divide the work / chores as equally as possible**. From researching destinations to planning days out to making money, both of you are responsible for making things happen. This also applies to the boring stuff like washing dishes, laundry, and so on.
- **Stay emotionally open and available**. It's too easy to get detached from friends and family in this digital nomad lifestyle.
- **Coordinate work time and play time**. We'll usually work on weekdays and travel on weekends… but there are also other routines to establish like getting groceries, going out for walks (sometimes together, sometimes solo), travel time, etc.
- **Embrace what makes you different**. My wife is an introvert, so I'll go to networking events by myself. What makes you and your partner different?

- **When crap happens, drop anything you have to in order to be there for your partner.** Again, I shouldn't have to say this, but it's just part of being a good partner. You may not *want* to return to their home country because of a funeral or an important family matter, but life doesn't always give us what we want.

The good news: on average, the 2nd person does not double your costs. You'll already have a place to stay, and can benefit from buying food or other items in slightly larger quantities. Expect each adult to add 50-80% to the first adult's cost. This means, of course, they'll need to pay their own way.

The bad news: their dreams may not necessarily be your dreams, and this is not something you can force on them. Have them go through the book and the worksheets to help clarify their interests, then have a sit-down with them to match up plans.

What if they still say 'no'? It's not fair for one partner to unilaterally make choices that affect both of you. If they're not on board, narrow down their objections or issues. Is it the place you're thinking of going? Are there issues related to their job? Are they afraid of something? Maybe they just need some time to warm up to the idea, or aren't as eager to leave their old life behind. Few situations will require you to choose between your partner and your travel plans, and a delay or wait may be necessary before they're on board.

Traveling with children

Important note: Nomads of all family types can make the digital nomad lifestyle work, including families with four or more children, single parents, same-sex parents, and many others. For examples and inspirations, go check out a list at becomingadigitalnomad.com/yes-you-can.

If you have children coming along, all the merrier! While younger children may not know what's going on or how unusual things are about to become, school-age kids may have already learned something of life's typical routines.

Bring up your future travels well in advance to give everybody time to get used to the idea. You might bring up the conversation of traveling by asking 'what-if' questions (e.g. 'What if we went traveling to a foreign country?'), or you might even make researching new countries or destinations a task for your children to do. Give them the chance to make some choices (like what toys to bring on the plane, or what sort of places you should see when you arrive). Expect them to be sad to leave their friends at first, but know that the rush of new experiences and adventures will soon replace those feelings. Some kids may rejoice in not having to go to a 'normal' or 'boring' school any more.

You may need to figure out how to get them out of school or otherwise handle the formalities of pulling them out. If this is just a test of the digital nomad lifestyle, it's likely easier to do when the school year is on break / holiday. If this isn't a test, you may need to make some choices on how best to educate your children while traveling. Families do this a lot of different ways, from 'unschooling' to 'worldschooling'. Either of these ways lets the world be their teacher instead of a formal curriculum. Homeschooling and worldschooling have come a long way, and videos teaching virtually any subject matter for almost any grade level can be found for free on the internet.

That said, it goes without saying that this will be a personal choice that you can customize for your children.

There are plenty of nomads that take their children with them as they travel:

- livingnomadstyle.com — Mandy, Chase, and their three sons traveled as a nomadic family from 2014 to 2017, and their archives make for some great reading.
- newschoolnomads.com — Jenn, Brent, two boys, and three pets have an entire category on homeschooling in their archives.
- carinaofdevon.wordpress.com — Martina, Julian, two daughters, and Carina of Devon (their boat). While they moved ashore in 2019 and no longer live on a boat, the seven years of archives offer plenty of tips and ideas for this lifestyle.
- nomadmomlife.com — Clara travels with her husband and two kids, but the focus here is on being a mother and nomad. Men, read this to understand what might be going on inside your wife's head.
- vagabondfamily.org — "built for parents or soon to be parents who want something different for themselves and their children. Living a travel (or nomadic) lifestyle throws a lot of challenges your way and we are here (as a group) to help you prepare, plan and live a less common lifestyle with your children."

Other resources for nomads traveling with kids include:
- worldschoolingcentral.com — highlighting nomad families, on-target blog posts, and plenty of solid advice. Join the Facebook group at facebook.com/groups/worldschoolingcentral.
- nomadtogether.com — Paul and Becky Kortman, along with their four kids, run a podcast, wrote a guidebook, and have created a community for nomad parents to connect. Join the Facebook group at facebook.com/groups/LocationIndependentFamilies.

- connectionseducation.com — potentially tuition-free online curriculum available through Pearson. Americans only, however.

Traveling for the LGBT community

Whether traveling solo or with your partner, a lot of the advice you've already read applies to you as well. Yes, there are countries and areas of the world you probably won't want to visit, but thankfully there's plenty of advice on where's safe.

Some resources specifically for LGBT travelers, and some LGBT digital nomads / travel bloggers worth reading:
- boundingoveroursteps.com — Mindy and her wife Ligeia have been married for over a decade and go vegan.
- dopesontheroad.com/ - Meg and Lindsay are a great inspiration regardless of who you are. The blog equips LGBT travelers to "live a life of adventures".
- globetrottergirls.com — since 2010, Dani is *the* globetrotting girl that "makes mistakes so you don't have to!". Currently a one-woman show, but has traveled with partners before.
- iglta.org — "The International Gay & Lesbian Travel Association was founded in 1983 and is the world's leading network of LGBTQ-welcoming tourism businesses."
- ilga.org/maps-sexual-orientation-laws — produces color-coded maps in several languages showing where being gay or lesbian is protected, recognized, or criminalized. A good indicator of where and where not to travel.
- indefiniteadventure.com — Sam and Zab are "a British couple with insatiable wanderlust" and are also vegans.
- minkaguides.com — Fanny Minka is "Part-time drag queen, Full-time travel content queen", and awesome.
- mynormalgaylife.com — Jose travels with his husband Alfred. Lots of blog posts of their travels.
- nomadicboys.com — Stefan and Sebastien's mission is to "seek out and showcase unique romantic, culinary and

outdoor adventures to inspire you to travel to places beyond the pink comfort zone."
- outtraveler.com — general travel news and stories emphasizing diversity and experiences.
- travelsofadam.com — one of the longest-running travel blogs kept by a gay traveler. Travel, lifestyle, and hipster guides galore.
- twobadtourists.com — David and Auston offer plenty of advice and city guides.
- wikitravel.org/en/Gay_and_lesbian_travel — an excellent one-page primer on where is safe or dangerous to travel.

Based on your research, it's time to pick the first place to go (and remember there will be plenty more in the future, so save all your research!). Start filling in the next worksheet with the details of your upcoming travels as they fit into place.

Worksheet #7: The plan

Date: _____

Find this at becomingadigitalnomad.com/worksheet7. Print a copy and complete offline, or complete online, then print or save.

Fill in the blanks to create your plan. We've talked about these questions for the last several pages, and now it's your time to answer them. Circle your choice of words that are in bold and fill in the blanks as appropriate.

I plan to go to _____ (city, country).

I chose this city because _____ .

I'm fluent / conversational / currently learning / a newbie in the local language.

I will live in a(n) host family house / co-living space / apartment / Airbnb.

I plan to stay there for **1 / 2 / 3 / 4 weeks / months**.

I have savings of _____ in the bank (note amount and currency).

I anticipate going on _____ (month and day), and I'll be getting there by **plane / bus / train / car**.

To make money, I plan to _____ .
I might also _____ .

I'll be going with my **spouse / life partner / traveling buddy / child(ren)** .

I already **have / have applied for** my passport.

I'll be **storing / selling / giving away** my car.

I'll be **storing / selling / giving away** my furniture.

Some questions I still need to answer include:

_____ .

Nomadus interruptus: just a test, please

This brief section is dedicated to those who just want to test the nomad lifestyle out. If you've already made the decision that you're going to become a nomad, then you can skip right to the next section. Otherwise, read on.

I haven't come across a lot of people talking about the best way to test the digital nomad lifestyle out for themselves, so let's take a few pages to set this up right. Be sure to fill in the worksheet at the end of the section to pull all your answers together.

Some people jump into the nomadic lifestyle with both feet. Sometimes it works for them, but it doesn't work for everyone. After all, what would happen if you quit your job, sold your car, and bought a one-way ticket to Thailand… and then realized you actually hated the lifestyle?

The bad news: It can happen.

The good news: Getting yourself in that situation is a completely avoidable issue.

Of all the steps to this Nomadus Interruptus test, this first step is the most important: **Set up a good, clean test environment.** If this test is going to give you the information you need, you have to make a clean break from your usual lifestyle, job, friends, family, and so on. Anyone not going with you needs to get used to staying in touch through phone calls and e-mails, since you won't be joining them for dinner.

A great way to think of this test is to picture the Neutral Buoyancy Laboratory in Houston, Texas. This lab is NASA's way of training future astronauts to work in a foreign environment, wearing a bulky spacesuit, and getting used to a different level of gravity. The lab holds 6.2 million gallons (23.4 million liters) of water, and is big enough to hold a full-size replica of their habitat in space along with the equipment they'll be using. Working underwater isn't a perfect substitute for the zero-gravity environment of space, but it's as close as they can get while on Earth.

Your test need not involve literally the biggest pool you've ever seen, and on that note, your test doesn't even have be to an exotic foreign country. The next state, province, or country over is fair game. **The goal here is to try a new pattern of life in a new location.** Get to know this new location in the short time you have and make it home. If your budget is severely limited, you could try house-sitting or house-swapping. The goal here is to adapt and do the sorts of things you'd want to do as a digital nomad.

Regardless of how the test turns out, remember that the digital nomad lifestyle does not require a full-time commitment. Be a part-time digital nomad six months out of the year, or during your kid's school break. It's entirely up to you.

The five questions of the Nomadus Interruptus test

As elsewhere in the book, there are a few questions to ask yourself, and there's a worksheet for you to write down your answers.

#1: What specific thing will you accomplish during this test?

Pick a specific *work-related* thing you'll get done during this test. Make this as specific as possible. Do you want to set up a website for a business, do some market research, or start offering a service during this test? Are you testing your ability to do remote work with your employer, get new clients of your own, or something else altogether?

#2: How much time can you spare?

Anywhere from a week to a month is a good amount of time — but base the length on how much time and money you're able to dedicate to this test. Maybe you've arranged to take the test as a remote worker for your company, or maybe you're taking this test while you're on vacation. Either is fair game.

However long you have, the goal is the same: to disconnect from your normal life (as best as possible!) and approach the lifestyle with as clean a slate as possible. Break from your usual routine. Get up later (or earlier), work a different schedule, explore a new area, and experience something new.

#3: How will you disconnect from your normal life?

Start with your desires and needs — a test like this is your chance to try almost anything. Of course, your needs (and the needs of your traveling companions) will have to be considered, along with the realities of moving somewhere new. If you have work commitments, they must be given priority as well to avoid going completely off the grid.

#4: Where should the test be held?

As said before, you don't have to go to another country for this test. At the very least, aim for a city in a different state or province that's at least a little different from where you live. Whether it's larger or more rural is up to you; just try to make it different in some way. Consider places you might have to fly to in order to best simulate the realities of packing for flying. If you opt to drive instead of fly, get a scale to weigh your luggage and pack everything inside to fit that weight limit.

#5: How will you pay for the test?

Whether it's savings or money made working, the money's gotta come from somewhere. Do not assume you will make any money from new businesses during this test, or that any money earned from new businesses will be received during your test. In other words, make sure you have a financial safety net. However, part of this test is so that you can find out how you will support yourself if you decide to do the real thing. **Don't treat this as a mini-vacation.**

Worksheet #8: Putting it all together for a test

Date: _____

Find this at becomingadigitalnomad.com/worksheet8. Print a copy and complete offline, or complete online, then print or save.

Fill in the blanks and circle the appropriate words or phrases that are in bold. See the previous section for more details about the questions.

#1: The specific thing I will accomplish during this test: _____ .

#2: I can spare _____ **days / weeks / months** for this test.

#3: I'll disconnect from my normal life by _____ .

#4: I plan to go to _____ (city, country).
I chose this location because _____ .

I will live in a(n) **host family house / co-living space / apartment / Airbnb**.

#5: I'll pay for this test with **my savings of** _____ (note amount and currency) / **my job** / **by** _____ .

To make money, I plan to _____ .
I might also _____ .

I **will / will not** be working with my current employer during the test.

I anticipate leaving on _____ (month and day), and I'll be getting there by **plane / bus / train / car**.

I'll be going with my **spouse / life partner / traveling buddy / child / children**.

I **have my passport / have applied for my passport / won't need a passport.**

During the test…

Follow the other sections of the book — there's plenty of advice on finding work, how to settle in, creating or getting into a new routine, and so on.

Some things to do or keep in mind during this test:
- Print off the previous worksheet (worksheet #8) and post it somewhere you'll see it on a regular basis.
- Be working towards your specific goal every working day.
- Remember that this lifestyle is not *just* about working — head out and meander when you can. Enjoy your new life!
- Remember this test is as much for your traveling companions as it is for you. Keep the lines of communication open to hear what's working and what's not.

No test can fully cover every aspect of the digital nomad lifestyle, but most people will get a sense of whether the lifestyle is for them or not. As long as you don't burn all your bridges after crossing them (a bad move, no matter your lifestyle), your options remain plentiful.

Now that the test is over...

Yep, there's another worksheet for that. There's also some responses to statements you might have made about your test.

Worksheet #9: post-test: how's it going?

Date: _____

Find this at becomingadigitalnomad.com/worksheet9. Print a copy and complete offline, or complete online, then print or save.

Complete this as soon after your test ends as possible. Answer each question with a rating from 1-10: 1 being 'completely disagree' and 10 being 'completely agree'. If you had a traveling companion for this test, get their answers separately, then compare your thoughts.

Statement	Disagree.....Agree
I settled into a new routine easily.	1 2 3 4 5 6 7 8 9 10
I kept to the routine I chose.	1 2 3 4 5 6 7 8 9 10
I was able to work with fewer interruptions.	1 2 3 4 5 6 7 8 9 10
I made new friends and networked.	1 2 3 4 5 6 7 8 9 10
I adapted to the new city well.	1 2 3 4 5 6 7 8 9 10
I stuck to my budget well.	1 2 3 4 5 6 7 8 9 10
I found time to explore the city.	1 2 3 4 5 6 7 8 9 10
I felt physically and emotionally stable.	1 2 3 4 5 6 7 8 9 10
I accomplished my goal from question 1.	1 2 3 4 5 6 7 8 9 10

What was your biggest win during this test?

_____

What was the biggest issue during this test?

_____

What's one thing that would have made one of your ratings above higher?

_____

What part of this test felt the easiest?

_____

What part of this test was the hardest to complete?

_____

How did your routine during this test differ from your routine at home?

_____

How productive did you feel while working?

_____

What did you miss from (or about) home?

_____

Was there a part of the lifestyle you didn't get to test?

_____

Do any of these statements fit how you felt?

- **I missed my family / my friends** — easily the biggest one for lots of people. You'll make new friends wherever you go. Many nomads remain close to their friends and family 'back home' by making time to catch up online, playing games together or just chatting on Skype.
- **I missed home** — the concept of 'home' changes as a nomad, so let's drill down to what you actually missed about home. Did you forget a favorite pillow? (Some nomads travel with theirs, and that's OK.) Was the place you chose to stay missing something important? (Consider it a part of the lifestyle to pick up and repurchase the things you want in your life.) Was it an emotional connection with some element of where you were before? Or did you simply miss the place you'd been living before? Nomads need not give up all their creature comforts, though some can be more difficult to take with you.
- **I didn't make enough money** — time to reconfigure and reconsider. Sure, you can live off savings for a while, but not indefinitely. Was your projected budget reasonably accurate? Were you spending more than you'd expected, or was income not coming in as you'd expected?
- **Moving all the time was hard** — it certainly can be. Many nomads take full advantage of the 90-day tourist visas available to them, while others may choose to stay in one place longer, thanks to a tourist visa extension or an entirely different visa altogether (think visas for work, education, retirement, business, etc.). The speed at which you travel from place to place is up to you.
- **I don't know where to go next** — OK, fair enough… but this is more of an excuse than a reason, especially this early on. Enjoy a place, then try a neighboring country or another place you liked from your research. There are around 200 different countries (depending on which listing you choose to follow) to take in, and in each of those are lots of options, from big cities to rural areas.
- **I prefer my old routine / lifestyle** — really? Which parts? This might be a reason to take a second test, albeit one

with the routine / lifestyle altered to suit your interests. Not every part of your life needs to be completely changed for a test like this, after all.
- **There was culture shock / a language barrier** — this is legitimate — but dealing with it is just a part of the nomadic lifestyle. Even after 10 years, it still happens to us. Once you're out of your home country, you're going to realize rather quickly how different other people's lives are. Plenty of tech and tools can help with the language barrier, though the initial culture shock when you arrive never completely disappears.
- **It just wasn't as much fun as expected** — to be sure, the nomadic lifestyle is one that requires work. That's typical for any sort of proactive lifestyle you choose, rather than one you just fall into. That said, what sort of fun did you miss? Was this a chance to join a local football / soccer team, to research the local board game cafes, or a good reason to find Facebook groups of fun people?

What if it's not for me?

If you love the idea of a digital nomad lifestyle but you've decided it's not for you, consider other ways of connecting with the world:
- **Become an Airbnb host** — you already know that our first choice for finding a place to live is always Airbnb. Sure, your city or neighborhood might look stodgy and boring to you, but just about everybody thinks that about where they live. Who knows? Your place might be perfect for a traveler.
- **Become a homestay host** — similar to offering an Airbnb, but this one gets you actively involved with your guests instead of simply offering a place. It's a great chance to show off your hometown, introduce the local cuisine, practice a foreign language you learned in high school, and basically connect with the digital nomad community and other travelers.

- **Offer to help the nomads you meet** — from storing their stuff to using your address to receive their mail or packages, having a stable address and place (or being more familiar with local customs or the local language) can be invaluable to a nomad. If you thought your city or country's bureaucracy was crazy, imagine going in without knowing what to do or not speaking the language!
- **Exchange houses** — you might not be ready or able to travel full-time, but offering your house on a housing exchange can give you the opportunity to holiday someplace far away. These sorts of exchanges will also enable someone to come to your place and look after your garden and pets.
- **Be a house-sitter** — another option to consider when you go on vacation, this can be a super-cheap way to see other parts of the world. Do take into consideration the potential limitations of a house-sit that I've listed, however.
- **Start an online business** — whether or not you leave your local community, an online business offers you a way to be in touch with clients or customers around the world. No, it's not the same as stepping out of your door into a brand-new environment every few weeks or months; but it can help you feel less like an isolated island and more like a global citizen.

Whatever your results and whatever your choice, I hope you found the Nomadus Interruptus test useful. Whether you plan to be a full-time digital nomad, a part-time one, or just plan to host digital nomads, the next section focuses on making money.

Step 3: Making money as a nomad

It's time to snap back to reality for a few pages. Unless you're independently wealthy or doing the nomad thing from your savings, you're going to have to make some money as you travel. As recently as ten years ago, this would have been a seriously uphill battle — the notion of working remotely has come a long way. While people were making the digital nomad lifestyle work a decade ago, it's really just been in the last few years or so that the lifestyle has achieved broad acceptance in the mainstream world.

When you're thinking about money, there's a very important element to keep in the back of your mind. It's the notion of **geo-arbitrage**: living in a country with a lower cost of living while making money online in a stronger currency (think US dollars, euros, or British pounds). Put another way, you want to work for relatively high wages from one country while living and spending a relatively small amount of money in another country. This is how nomads can afford to live on what some might consider a much lower income, and why most nomads don't work locally. If you live in, say, New York, you might need $3,000 a month to live comfortably. Get to Bangkok or Medellin, and you might quickly realize you can live on around $1,000 a month. Get to Chiang Mai and you might be able to live on $500 a month. (Do note, of course, that your ability to do this will be based cutting costs to a minimum. Start eating out or partying a bunch and your cost of living may be as high as it was before.)

When it comes to making money online, there are no silver bullets, no get-rich-quick schemes, and no sustainable shortcuts. There *are*, however, a ton of ways to make money while traveling. So long as you don't have to physically touch someone or be in the same room as the person you're working with, you can probably find an opportunity to make money. **The biggest thing to remember is to be proactive**. Waiting for opportunities to find you is the wrong way to fly.

Working as a digital nomad means you'll be following at least one of these four paths:

- Consultant — offer advice, counseling, or information to clients.
- Employee — make stuff or offer a service for your employer.
- Entrepreneur — run your own business, making products or providing services.
- Freelancer — take gigs and deliver a product / service in order to be paid.

A quick word on flag theory

Since 'flag theory' comes up every so often in talks about money and the nomadic lifestyle, let's give it the brief introduction it deserves. The term 'flag theory' dates back to 1964 and is from a book by novelist and investment pundit Harry D Schultz. In essence, flag theory is a diversification strategy to protect your money, increase your privacy, pay fewer (or no) taxes, and retain as much freedom as possible.

A proponent of flag theory will 'plant their flag' in several countries. They'll have (or get) a passport from one country, be a resident of another country, have a bank account in a third country, and potentially have their business incorporated in a fourth country. Each of these choices are made based on how taxes are handled, how you or your money are treated, what the tax rates are, what red tape or bureaucracy must get involved, how well your privacy is protected in these countries, the fees or charges, how many options are offered, and so on.

The more 'flags' mentioned in the flag theory you read about, the more countries you choose to involve (and the more complicated things can get). Someone practicing this theory might also have a 'playground' country with no or low sales tax where they spend their money, or they might host their website in a country with strong privacy or anonymity laws, for example.

If you have a net worth of more than $100,000, flag theory is almost certainly worth the time and effort. It's important to remember, of course, that you're still complying with the rules and laws (and the loopholes) of the countries your flags are in. Is your net worth between $50,000 and $100,000? It's worth researching, but you might find the fees and setup costs are more than what flag theory might save you. Under $50,000? You might still want to research flag theory further for the freedom it may provide you, but you're less likely to see much in the way of savings.

The intricacies of flag theory go beyond the scope of this book, and the best options seem to change from one day to the next. Among other websites, head to escapeartist.com, flagtheory.com, and nomadcapitalist.com for information on planting your flags around the world. These websites, and others like them, often have a less-than-rosy outlook on world governments, so do your own research before choosing a plan.

Personally? I prefer the pragmatic approach — don't fire your government, but do give it a report card. Look for ways to legally reduce the amount of taxes you pay, and look at things like bank accounts or investment accounts with a fine-toothed comb. Renouncing your citizenship (especially as an American) and acquiring another citizenship are two time-consuming and expensive processes. Going where you and your money are treated best is a great mindset, but keeping things simple wins the day for me, unless there's a good reason to make things more complicated. Most first-world countries are quickly tightening their laws to make slipping through financial loopholes harder — again, do your own research.

Working with your existing job

While a significant percentage of nomads are entrepreneurs or freelancers that take gigs, many are considered 'remote workers' by their employer. If you fall into the latter category, working within the guidelines of your company and your boss are critical to making the arrangement work for everyone. Things like a general schedule, any conference calls or company-wide meetings you need to attend, and how you'll get paid (if that changes) are all important considerations to work out. This will be unique to each nomad and employer, so take the time to work this out well before your departure date.

A few other considerations to think about when working remotely:
- What do co-workers need to do to adapt to your transition? If you were having weekly meetings before, will you keep to those same times?
- What security measures do you need to take? Good password management is a given, but there may be IT or corporate guidelines you'll be expected to follow. If you're one of the first remote workers in your company, you may have a hand in creating them for yourself.
- What hours of the day will you be available for immediate response? Will you be expected to work 'office hours' on the company's time zone, or does your schedule change when you change countries?
- Can you handle things on a flexible basis, or do you need to dedicate a set number of hours to work? Is overtime or 'crunch time' necessary, and how will that work?

Working on your own

Work is definitely an important element to sustaining the nomad lifestyle, but it's only part of the equation here — don't make this nomadic journey *entirely* about work. Too many nomads I've met have spent so much time focusing on the work part that they forget why they wanted to be nomads. As you might remember from step 1, each person's reasons will be different, but I've never met a nomad that wanted to spend all of their time and energy working a job.

Whether you're working remotely for a company or working independently, getting your workspace set up is important, as is making it as comfortable as you can. Your office chair might be a dining room chair instead of a classy, office chair with wheels, but let's focus on what you *need*, not what you *want*. If the table / desk isn't quite the right height, use some shims (thin pieces of wood) to adjust it to just the right height. If you need a laptop at a different height to prevent 'laptop neck', buy a laptop stand or discover how versatile a stack of books can be.

If I'm working 'from home,' how do I keep from getting distracted online? In Tim Ferriss' *Four-Hour Workweek*, he described practicing 'selective ignorance' and maintained a 'low-information diet'. He would read the front-page headlines through the newspaper machines, ask people what's new in the world, and otherwise allowed dependable people to help him make decisions on things like voting. How people get their news has changed quite a bit since that book came out in 2007, of course.

Instead of telling you to stay 'selectively ignorant', I propose a 'low-fat information diet' that challenges you to use a limited amount of time on social media or to keep up with the news however you like. Here's how it works:
- Pick a specific time (and amount of time) every day to read the news, social media, mess around online, whatever.

- This might be 30 minutes starting at 11am, an hour starting at 1pm, 15 minutes at the start of your day, or whenever suits you. Just make it a specific length and a specific time each workday — barring some emergency or other very good reason, this will be your *only* opportunity each day to do this.
- To time yourself, use a kitchen timer, a free tool like RescueTime (rescuetime.com), a free app like selfcontrolapp.com (for Macs only) or SnapTimer (for Windows), a Chrome add-on like StayFocusd, or a Firefox add-on like LeechBlock NG. The goal is the same: be aware of how much time is passing as you're doing something.
- As you're beginning to time yourself, it will be worth asking yourself whether a given website is worth a part of that limited time. Will *not* visiting this website negatively affect you in some way? Will going to this website take you down an internet rabbit hole that only wastes time?
- One of my biggest struggles has been Facebook, especially when some political or news event gets people riled up. Beyond the obvious advice of 'don't feed the trolls' I can't always follow myself, click the '...' in the upper-right and choose from the options to hide, unfollow, or snooze the offender. Aim to take that action against the *source*, not your Facebook friend themselves (unless, of course, they're the ones typing the incendiary comments or posts). Unfriending and blocking remain last-resort options, and letting go of some contacts may be what's needed.
- When the timer rings, take a few minutes to clear your mind (or grab another cup of coffee), then get back to work.

What about e-mail? Few e-mails require instant responses. Aim to check e-mail a few times a day, then close the tab / browser once done. If necessary, a virtual assistant can be empowered to handle your e-mails and forward those that require your attention.

Co-working spaces

Co-working spaces are predictable places to find desks, office chairs, fast internet, and an entrepreneurial group of people like you as you travel. They're places to get stuff done. Most offer a wide variety of packages, but the better deals are reserved for those who sign a longer-term contract. The space is often a built-in offline social network as well, since there are usually plenty of events happening on-site (or nearby) — but events and work rarely happen at the same time.

Some people love co-working spaces and look for them as soon as they arrive somewhere, while others don't really need or bother with them. Personally, we book Airbnb's that offer plenty of space to work and live so that no co-working space is necessary. Of course, even if you have the space to work wherever you're staying, you still might find a co-working space to be preferable for the people, the networking, or just a change of pace.

Whichever side you're on, these are great places to know about, thanks to the social functions and the pool of talent that exists there. Need someone to Photoshop something or give something a second look? There's probably someone around at your local co-working space who can help out as a favor. Remember you're part of a community, so give as much as you take. Even if you're a non-member (or a just-for-the-day sort of member), you can often hang out in the public / common areas, get to know the people that work there, hear about cool projects long before they're making news, and find people that can do what you need done.

Co-working spaces do have a few unwritten rules, of course:
- People are there to work, first and foremost. While a casual, quiet, and short conversation is bound to be fine with most people, anyone wearing headphones or earbuds is usually sending a clear 'do not disturb' sign.

- Don't assume the people there are interested in brainstorming, having their brains picked, or 'talking shop'.
- It's generally fine to mention what you're making, but never try to 'hard sell' anyone.
- Take your phone calls off the working floor (preferably *not* in an echo-filled area), and in general keep the volume down.
- Remember these are shared spaces, so unless you've paid for a dedicated spot, that spot isn't 'yours'. First come, first serve.

New co-working spaces are opening all the time, and the best ones are usually found through word of mouth. To get you started, see several major worldwide chains and a few directories to help you find the independent co-working spaces close to you:
- copass.org — work at 950 spaces around the world with one monthly membership. Has a few different plans based on how often you use co-working spaces.
- coworker.com — "13,000+ available coworking spaces in 170 countries. Find and book yours today." Find spaces near beaches, rural escapes, places that are female-focused, and so on.
- impacthub.net — a chain of almost 100 'hub' co-working spaces around the world. Focused on global Sustainable Development Goals to view their impact on the world.
- onecoworking.com — "Access to the best coworking spaces in your city and around the world with one app and one membership!". Most locations are in Europe, though six continents are represented on the map.
- opencoworking.org — this non-profit founded in 2012 offers a thing called the Coworking Visa that allows members of one co-working space to enter another co-working space for free for a limited number of days. See a world map at the predictably-named coworkingvisamap.com.
- regus.com — claiming 3,000 locations in 900 cities and 120 countries, there's a good chance there's one close to where you are right now.

- startupblink.com/coworking — offers a worthy map of over 1,500 co-working spaces around the world.
- wework.com — around 300 buildings in 62 cities, with the vast majority in the US, Western Europe, and China.
- workfrom.co — a large directory of co-working spaces, coffee shops, restaurants, and other places to work from.

So, what *do* you do to make money?

The great news about digital nomads is the variety of work available. We're almost to the point where anything that *can* be done remotely *is* being done remotely by someone out there. So long as you don't have to be in a specific physical location or physically touch something or someone, it's a possibility.

I feel compelled to note a few things as we begin this section:
- I have not tried every single strategy listed in this book — there's a ton of stuff listed here, for crying out loud. Each and every one of these has been mentioned by nomads as a way they've made money, and I've linked to nomads that write about doing that thing online where possible. What you do and how well you do will vary based on your skills, effort, a bit of luck, and plenty of other things.
- It's worth remembering the reason why you want to become a digital nomad — and it isn't just to work. Work is a necessary part of the nomadic lifestyle, but it's not *the* reason people become nomads. At the end of the day, it's about freedom to live your life your way.
- Whatever may be happening in the rest of your nomad journey, **be professional in all communications and avoid missing deadlines at all costs.** 'Radio silence' is perhaps the biggest cardinal sin a nomad can make when it comes to their clients. Your boss and/or your clients don't care that you're in Bali — they care that their needs are being met for the price they're willing to pay. If you're not doing that, you're slowing them down or costing them money.

- Time zones — and daylight savings time — are crucial things to remember. If you're scheduling a conference or Skype call, triple-check the time zones to avoid that awkward moment when you're an hour early (or late!). Use worldtimebuddy.com, timeanddate.com, or Google '[city] time' to figure out what time it is there relative to where you are.
- As you're looking at the following options. the big thing to remember here is to focus on solid, honest, valuable work. Don't bother with get-rich-quick schemes or multi-level marketing schemes (MLM's) where getting other people to sell the product pays more than selling the product itself.
- Watch for contractual obligations and non-compete clauses, especially if you've been in the freelance world. Don't try to steal clients or work from your current employer. Beyond being a breach of your contract, it's some seriously bad karma.

The list of opportunities

This is the most complete list of digital nomad jobs that I know of, but no list can ever be completely exhaustive. Your skills, desires, education, and experiences will prepare you more for some occupations than others, so you'll need to peruse the list thoroughly to find the ones that work for you.

Some of the descriptions may sound simple if you're already familiar with the industry. It's meant as a basic list to give you a sense of whether an occupation is worth further research, not a full-fledged job description.

Sales and marketing

The sky's the limit here — since the field is *so* varied, it's just a matter of what you want to sell or market, or deciding to help someone else sell their stuff.
- **Affiliate marketing** — use or create channels (like social media, a blog, or a website) to offer affiliate links to appropriate audiences. Look at Kickbooster (a program for promoting Kickstarter projects), other people's e-books, local goods, or just about anything with an affiliate program.
- **eCommerce** — make an online store using shopify.com, etsy.com, and sell almost anything you can. Among others, see https://farawild.com/ for some seriously awesome products for women.
- **Marketing consultant** — help clients plan and execute marketing strategies, ideally in fields you're knowledgeable about or have experience with.
- **Performance (PPC - pay-per-click) marketer** — create, test, and find the best-performing ads for clients.
- **Public Relations** — greet the public, speak on behalf of a company, generate fresh ideas for marketing campaigns, and so on.

- **Vendor** — whether you're selling stuff on the street, in a market, or at festivals, this is the offline version of sales and marketing. Bonus points if they're your own products, of course!

Teaching jobs

There are lots of synonyms for 'teaching' here. Whether you're helping a five-year-old learn their ABC's or counseling a fifty-something to confront their emotional dark side, there's a role for you. The goal here is to help humans be better humans, however you do that.

- **Coaching / mentoring** — help people lose weight, start businesses, make websites, or a thousand other things. Start with sessions on Skype, Google Hangouts, Zoom, Facebook Messenger, or consider full platforms like satoriapp.com, coachingcloud.com, or jigsawbox.com.
- **Course creator** — record videos to break down processes on how to do things. The technical details behind making great videos can take some time to get right, but once you do, platforms like skillshare.com, udemy.com, and teachable.com help people find you.
- **Dance classes** — a great offline way to make some money, stay in shape, and meet people. Often arranged proactively at local bars or clubs, and sometimes done under the table.
- **English** — a very common subject for native or fluent English speakers to teach online or offline. Offline full-time jobs may move you into the 'expat' category in many countries, while some countries will want you to have TEFL / TESOL certification. Be aware that if you're American and the country you want to work in requires a federal-level background check, it may take weeks (or months!) to receive. Some part- or full-time jobs will have you teach students one-on-one online — a few include t.vipkid.com.cn, abc360.com, italki.com, verbalplanet.com and verbling.com.

- **Fitness classes** — whether you want to teach Pilates, Zumba, a bootcamp, or engage in some other heart-pumping action, you might be able to teach some classes. Market to the expats / nomads in the area, perhaps and/or partner with a local studio to use their space.
- **Lesson design** — make lessons, worksheets, or create other content to help other teachers. These materials will have come from your own personal teaching experience, so you'll obviously have to have done some teaching beforehand. While not specific to digital nomads, teacherspayteachers.com is a platform to sell your materials to other teachers.
- **Music** — Share your skills by tutoring or by working full-time at a school that teaches music. Play an instrument? Consider tutoring it.
- **Personal training** — create diet, exercise, or workout plans, meet with clients online or offline, and help people create their best body. See nerdfitness.com and maxwellsc.com as two examples of successful nomads, or trainerize.com as a platform to offer advice to clients.
- **Public speaking** — having an authoritative amount of experience in some field, along with having something valuable to say, can make gigs appear and doors open. See danniefountain.com, legalnomads.com/courses-speaking, and a whole lot of relevant speakers at dnxglobal.com.
- **SCUBA diving / Surfing** — It's always summertime somewhere, and getting certified to teach SCUBA diving puts you in a place to do what you love and teach it to others. Teach the hobby, how to use the equipment, safety, signals, navigation, and so on. Head to padi.com to get officially certified.
- **Ski / snowboarding** — prefer winter sports? Teach people how to ski or snowboard, take seasonal jobs around the slopes, or do your work between sessions on the hill. These gigs won't be year-round jobs, so get looking for jobs in the Northern Hemisphere from August to October (for jobs that will run roughly from October-March) and in

the Southern Hemisphere from January to March (for jobs that will run roughly from March-September). Find jobs at nzsia.org/job-vacancies, jobs.basi.org.uk, or take courses with wearesno.com or easkiandsnowboard.com to get qualified to teach.
- **Yoga teacher** — a surprisingly common occupation of digital nomads. Teach various classes, lead excursions, and stay flexible and healthy. Combine with any number of other healthy living gigs. Several examples of nomads making it work: theyoganomads.com, dutchsmilingyogi.com, happyyogatravels.com, and lindsaynova.com.

I'm a people person!
Focus less on the technical aspects and more on the people side of things.

- **Consultant** — use your expertise to create value, and use testimonials from previously satisfied customers to get more. You will need technical knowledge relevant to the subject, but I've listed it here because it's the human connection your clients are paying for.
- **Counselor / psychologist** — help other nomads handle any emotional or psychological issues they may have. This is not a job for everyone, as some formal schooling and experience may be required to be licensed in your home country. sonia-jaeger.com is one nomad doing this.
- **Customer service** — the sky's the limit here, since plenty of companies need people to serve their customers. Your job might be accomplished via e-mail, live chat, phone, or some other way.
- **Public relations** — be the spokesperson for a company whenever the media comes calling. Be ready for early-morning wake-up calls and putting out fires at any given time.
- **Spiritual leader / advisor** — exact offerings will vary based on religion or spirituality, but see Siete Saudades,

Lord Mercenary of The Myriad at themyriadhouseprime.com as one example.
- **Virtual assistant** — be someone's right-hand person. Exact responsibilities will vary, but may include social media posts, sending or responding to e-mails, scheduling meetings, researching, making travel arrangements, and so on. Expect to earn an hourly or monthly wage according to your skills and negotiated contract.

Technical jobs

To be sure, almost every digital nomad position relies in some way on your computer and having access to the internet in some way. Technical jobs are likely to require a better internet connection and more time spent on the computer than the average job.
- **App creation** — creating apps for Android or the iOS market requires a serious understanding of the market and how to make apps. It's a popular occupation for digital nomads, whether they work for themselves or companies. One example is run by Peter Lakatos and Beatrice Krell over at appnomads.com.
- **Coder / Computer programmer / Software developer** — write code, make stuff. This is a huge field for digital nomads, mainly because it can be done anywhere in the world. Some may specialize in a language or use case, while others may aim to improve their skills at coding boot camps or self-learning. For some, the highlight is that your skill shines through (or glosses over) any issues with formal education. See typicalprogrammer.com as one example, while fulltimenomad.com has a good getting-started guide.
- **Cryptocurrency mining** — process cryptocurrency transactions and potentially make some for yourself in the process. We're well past the days where a random person with a laptop could mine Bitcoin. Yes, there are other coins that can be mined with a laptop, whether it's a high-end gaming laptop or one that's a few years old… but today's serious miners aren't using laptops.

- **Cryptocurrency trader / investor** — trade cryptocurrencies on any of the online markets. This is quite possibly a match made in digital nomad heaven. It does require some knowledge about the industry, and the entire industry should not be considered anything other than high-risk. You shouldn't invest any more than you're willing to lose due to the many hazards.
- **Daytrading** — follow the news and trade stocks based on trends and swings. This definitely isn't for everyone, but if you've put in the time to learn technical analysis and can stay on top of the market, this might be a lucrative profession. It's also one where you can lose your pants real quick, so be aware of that as well. See the wanderingtrader.com.
- **Dropshipping** — one part marketing, one part customer service, and two parts setting up relationships with companies that actually store and ship the goods to your customers. A good business model for nomads, since all the physical work is done by others. johnnyfd.com has done it for years, and Anton's course dropshiplifestyle.com is considered one of the best training programs around, though it's expensive.
- **FBA (Fulfillment by Amazon)** — acquire, create, or have stuff made to order, then ship it to one of Amazon's warehouses for them to fulfill orders when they come in. Be aware this business can have some fairly significant start-up costs (think inventory, Amazon fees, etc.)
- **SEO optimizer / expert** — get paid to put people's websites on page one of search results. This can take a lot of technical skill to do well, but also requires some people skills to explain what you're doing or the results you're getting them. Get the experience on your own sites, take some courses, or work for a discount to get some testimonials under your belt.
- **System admin / Server maintenance** — fix problems on the server level for clients. Definitely a higher-level position for the experienced nomad, and not a job you can just jump into. This job may require some unusual hours and

being able to connect to a computer or tablet at a moment's notice, so you can't go too far off the grid.
- **Technical support** — whether you're telling clients to turn it off and back on again or trying to replicate a reported bug, this job requires both computer / product knowledge and a bit of compassion / customer service.
- **UX / UI designer** — Whether you're designing the User eXperience or User Interface of a website or app, you play an influential role in how an app, website, or service looks and feels. This can take some education and / or experience to get good at.
- **Website design / development** — make websites for people that want them. Most web designers stick with WordPress because it's simple to get started, and most package their services with the hosting and domain name. This is a very common occupation, and some nomads will partner with other nomads to offer a more complete package (such as graphic / logo design, content writing, etc.)
- **Website management / security / optimization** — maintain the website you built for a client, or manage a website created by someone else. These are good services to offer if you made the site and they usually have a good profit margin.

Artsy jobs for the creative types
- **Actor / Impersonator / Model** — you may have heard some stories about 'rent a foreigner' programs in China, where companies hire non-Chinese people to give an international appearance to an event or company. Other countries will cast non-locals for their language skills, their looks, or for any number of other reasons. Your best bet here is to keep networking, learn some of the local language, and be willing to audition for gigs at a moment's notice. Doing related work for local companies gets your foot in the door. Be sure to mention your language skills, but watch out for scams.

- **Artist** — there are a million ways to create art, and some are easier than others as a nomad. Creating murals, illustrations, and other scenes in exchange for meals or places or stay is one thing, but getting paid is (usually) a bit more challenging. Getting into painting, for example, means having to figure out a way to obtain paints and canvases, then transport your works with you until you sell them. Digital artists have an easier time, but artists of all kinds can find an audience on deviantart.com and artstation.com. Some nomadic artists to look up include homsweethom.com, krishancoupland.co.uk, derekalvarezart.com, and alexmathers.net.
- **Drone video producer** — it may be one tool in the videographer's suitcase, but a solid drone offers a dramatic perspective on the world. Be aware that a growing number of countries and regions are officially restricting or prohibiting the use of drones. One excellent resource to keep track of these rules is at drone-traveller.com, but the forums for your brand of drone would be a good place to research limitations as well.
- **Game developer (board, card, or video)** — whatever kind of game you want to make, there's a publisher to find or a bunch of details to set up. You might want to pitch to a publisher and let them do some of the mechanical stuff, or you might find yourself making games independently and using Kickstarter to fund their production. This is something I do over at entrogames.com, though I don't (currently) talk much about combining the digital nomad lifestyle with the gaming lifestyle.
- **Graphic designer** — make words come to life, or just make the boxes, bags, book covers, logos and other things that you're hired to make. See medium.com/nomad-designers or creativenomad.design.
- **Interior Designer** — make living spaces beautiful, suggest colors, or just talk about *feng shui*. You may need to connect with service providers to actually execute the plan, but the personal recommendations and styles can be given in many different ways.

- **Livestreamer** — related to video creator below, but your talent (be it video games, reviewing things, talking about stuff or something similar) is more 'live' and less 'edited'. It can be a technical field, and can be tough to get started in, but you get paid to do something you love. Plenty of people are on twitch.tv and Youtube, among other platforms.
- **Making jewelry or crafts** — some nomads do this using local materials to save on costs, make things look more exotic, or maybe even to charge more for the end product. You'll need to stay on top of production, shipping, customer service, and any number of details that can be more challenging while traveling. You might choose to work with locals, having them create the jewelry or crafts while you focus on the marketing and fulfillment. Sell your offerings on Etsy, eBay, or your own website. One example: 22stars.com.
- **Musician** — whether you're busking, performing in a band, DJ'ing, or are recording projects, there are plenty of opportunities to make a name for yourself while traveling. One great example: janekgwizdala.com.
- **Performers** — belly dance, hip hop, hula hoop, poi, and burlesque performers may have an uphill battle to live the nomadic lifestyle. On one hand, anything 'exotic' like this may be a natural fit for the events and festivals in the areas where you travel. On another, teaching and performing may have you going where the work is, not necessarily where you want to be.
- **Photography** — take photos for stock sites, on contract for publications, for assignments, or for sale to your fans. Photography licensing is also something to consider, and there are entire books written about it. You might also offer classes or tours where you take people to your favorite spots, or you might help Airbnb hosts get good pictures of their places. Some nomads doing photography include brendansadventures.com, neverendingmagic.com, and blamethemonkey.com. A few platforms to check out

include shotzyapp.com, snappr.co, scoopshot.com, photosesh.com, and photographercentral.com.
- **Podcast editor / Producer** — start each episode with a custom little message, a quick 'sponsored by' blurb, and you're on! Alright, there's a lot more to it than that. Find a niche you're passionate about, invite people to record, and get them talking about a mutual interest.
- **Tattoo artists** — get invited to shops or work with local shops once you've established your credibility.
- **Video creator, editor, uploader AKA vlogger** — make travel videos for the masses. Several notable vloggers among many, many others: Chris the Freelancer, Vagabrothers, PsychoTraveller, and itsatravelod.com.
- **Voice work** — record the voices for voice overs, commercials, cartoons, audiobooks, trailers, podcasts, training videos, and so on. For obvious reasons you'll need a good microphone and a very quiet space. Know what to charge by looking at globalvoiceacademy.com/gvaa-rate-guide. Look for work at actorsaccess.com, snaprecordings.com, stage32.com, voice123.com, voicebunny.com, or acx.com, if you want to focus on audiobooks. One nomad making it work is voicethatfrenchie.com.

Pound-the-keyboard jobs

These gigs will have you attached to the keyboard, but some won't always require the internet. Being a digital nomad means you never want to be too far from the internet, of course.

- **Advertising** — whether selling it on your own site or setting it up for other people, selling or managing ads can be a great overlap with other projects.
- **Affiliate sales** — match the products available with the audience. Simple, right? It can be a tough time finding the right match, not coming off as a shill, and staying on top of which programs and products are available. Oh, and ensuring you get paid fairly and accurately. Pair this with blogging, vlogging, or writing on sites you control. Among others, two masters of affiliate sales are Michelle Schroeder-Gardner of makingsenseofcents.com and Sharon Gourlay of digitalnomadwannabe.com.
- **Ambassadorships / Brand partnerships** — where advertising and affiliate campaigns are short-term, ambassadorships or brand partnerships are usually longer-term (three to six months, or even longer). These aren't as common as they used to be, but they're still around. Pair this with other writing gigs, and aim to be picky about which partnerships you take.
- **Author** — write a worthwhile book and sell it. Some will say the market is saturated with self-published books, but a good book with good marketing and a good plan can still succeed. Combine with blogging, vlogging, or another gig where you're doing a lot of writing.
- **Blogging** — people have written entire books about how to blog while traveling, so I won't pretend a paragraph will cover it. Whatever your topic of interest / passion, your blog becomes your platform and your soapbox. Make money with ads, affiliate links, ambassadorships, sponsored posts, and so on. See bloggingpro.com/jobs, or jobs.problogger.net to look for blogging jobs.
- **Community manager** — support a business by being part of their public face. That can mean keeping the social

media channels clean from spammers, asking the community questions, handling issues, planning events, and so on. The exact responsibilities will vary by company, naturally.

- **Data entry** — probably one of the more boring jobs on the list, and because it's considered lower-skill, it's also lower-paying. Since they're typically set up to be 'work-from-home' jobs, however, 'home' can be almost anywhere. Find these gigs on Guru.com, PeoplePerHour.com, Upwork.com, and elsewhere.
- **E-book creator** — assist authors in turning their manuscript into a compatible e-book file for Amazon, Apple, B&N, and so on. A bit of technical work, but an important step some need help with.
- **Editing / Proofreading** — much like freelance writing jobs, freelance editing jobs can have you working on almost any subject. Most agencies will expect you to take a test, then possibly edit a sample. It might be easier to find clients as you travel because you'll spot opportunities for editing / proofreading. It's just a matter of convincing the client to pay you.
- **Expert in something** — some websites will pay you money to answer other people's questions. JustAnswer.com, Studypool.com, Prestoexperts.com, and Experts123.com are a few. Others, like Ether.com, 6ya.com, Maven.co, and Clarity.fm, have you answer questions via phone instead of typing them.
- **Freelance writing / Copywriting** — another common gig that can let you go a thousand different ways based on your interests and skills. Write articles for newspapers or magazines, some marketing copy, financial reports, and lots of other stuff — you never really know what somebody might want / need. Among many other sites to find work: upwork.com, fiverr.com, and allfreelancewriting.com/freelance-writing-jobs.
- **Ghostwriter** — contract with someone else to tell their story, but let them put their own name on the cover as the author. Part of your job might be to organize the client's

thoughts into the most logical story to tell, or you might simply edit and improve the client's words.
- **Medical transcriptionist / Medical coder** — type out or code what you hear. The difference in what you earn can be months of training, completion of required certifications, and a lot more six-syllable words. 1dad1kid.com is one nomad who did it.
- **Mock online juror** — *wait, what?* This is basically a survey job to be part of an online focus group. This isn't going to be much more than going-out money at best, but it's pretty easy work. See onlineverdict.com for more.
- **Namer of things** — always thinking of the perfect names for things? Companies and individuals starting projects pay money for the perfect name. squadhelp.com and namingforce.com will accept your naming ideas for their contests. They offer free signup and free submission of your best suggestions, and the prizes can be enough to pay some bills.
- **Niche websites** — niche websites have one job, essentially: offering useful and interesting information on a very specific topic. Niche websites may be built to rank for certain, specific keywords ('best travel backpack', for example) The person that creates niche websites will typically engineer every page to be a near-perfect fit for a specific keyword or phrase. They may also add ads, affiliate links, or a storefront to make money from it. nichehacks.com and nichepursuits.com are two excellent resources.
- **Resume / CV writer** — there's definitely an art in making people look good on paper. Meet with clients via e-mail or video to discuss their needs, goals, and experience. Talk with them and deliver a Word document or PDF.
- **Social media management** — this can involve creating the posts, pins, and pictures for a client. If you have a good sense of what works on social media (and you're willing to stay on top of a fast-moving market), businesses will pay to have a professional to manage things for them.

- **Transcriptionist** — type out what you hear. You'll want a seriously accurate (and high) words per minute rate to complete jobs quickly to make it worth your while. Head to rev.com, transcribeme.com or gotranscript.com (among others).
- **Translator** — translate between languages you know as a fluent or native. The best practice in the industry is to translate *from* the language you've learned *into* your native language. You might take some jobs the other way around, but the chances of getting some subtleties mixed up is higher. Use your CAT (computer-assisted translation) tool of choice, such as Trados Studio, MemoQ, or a word processor like Microsoft Word or Google Docs to translate a source document. Proz.com is really the first and best stop to get started — take your time to get to know the site and complete your profile.
- **Website usability testing** — test people's websites and give your thoughts on how to make them better. Use software to record your screen, then add a microphone to add your feedback. Head to usertesting.com or trymyui.com to sign up for a couple of similar services.

Money and legal jobs

- **Accountant** — help people or small businesses keep their incomes and expenses straight. Use tools like QuickBooks, FreshBooks, Xero, and so on to organize your client's expenses. See digitalnomadaccounting.com for a nomad serving nomads.
- **Tax preparer** — a more complex job, but a more lucrative one if you can handle multiple international systems of taxes and regulations. Licenses or permits may be required to call yourself a tax preparer, depending on the country.
- **Financial advisor** — call it 'wealth management' if you like, but a financial advisor makes sure your money is making money. Aim for a CFP (Certified Financial Planner - learn more at cfp.net) certification so people know they're

working with a professional. See xyplanningnetwork.com or nomadfinancial.com.
- **Lawyer** — today you learned you can be a lawyer and a nomad! Give legal advice without that annoying 'I am not a lawyer' disclaimer. A nomad making it work is over at hashtag-legal.com.

Help people travel better
- **Work with surfing, scuba, skiing, snowboarding, or other tour agencies** — sell their packages or refer people to their shops online or offline. This is a good one to combine with blogging, vlogging, affiliate sales, and so on.
- **Photograph their honeymoon or vacation** — as a local of sorts, you're already on the scene to capture a special moment in their lives. Create a portfolio and get the ball rolling on a platform like Flytographer, or create your own website.
- **Travel planner** — most anyone who's traveled to a place might serve as a travel planner — give recommendations on where to stay, what to see, how to get around, and so on. You might make a specific, unique itinerary for the client based on their interests, and you might also make bookings on their behalf. Unlike a more traditional travel agent (who only makes money from commissions), a travel planner may work for planning fees and / or commissions.
- **Tour guide** — it might be a little cheeky being a tour guide in a place you've only been at for a short time, but you might find a gig helping to translate, partnering with a local, or scouting out your own tour. Tour guides also work wherever their company sends them, meaning your travel is more likely to be paid for. Researching skills and customer service skills are essential.

Offline service jobs

Yes, yes, I remember what the term 'digital nomad' means — someone who works digitally and lives nomadically. Jobs in this category fall into the 'find jobs online, deliver services offline'. As far as I'm concerned, anything that lets you keep traveling counts! These gigs might complement an income made online or might make a trip somewhere new more viable.

A warning with this category: Although most online jobs can pass the test of 'not competing with locals', these jobs may compete with locals offering the same services. Governments (and locals) don't necessarily like the competition, so tread a little more carefully here and be prepared to get work visas or permits if necessary. That'll usually allow you to stay for longer

- **Au pair / Childcare / Nanny** — care for children in their home or in another pleasant setting. You'll have better luck if you're younger and female, and your schedule may not always allow for lots of traveling time. See greataupair.com, aupair.com, and aupairworld.com as a few places to start looking for jobs.
- **Barista / Bartender** — you didn't become a digital nomad just to serve coffees or beers, but they can be decent jobs that you can find just about anywhere. Although they might not require a lot of experience or training, be aware of local 'responsible service of alcohol' requirements if you plan to sling cocktails. Short term work is more likely to be under-the-table work.
- **Beautician** — offer manicures, pedicures, facials, aromatherapy sessions, and so on at your home, as an on-call or house-call service, or perhaps even at parties. This is most likely a part-time gig, unless you have an excellent way of networking.
- **Cruise ship work** — a cruise ship is a microcosm of the world, which is a nice way of saying there are plenty of types of jobs on a cruise ship — hundreds or even thousands of workers on every ship. The accommodations

for staff are unlikely to be the largest, and you may find you're expected to stay on board as the paying customers go ashore at port. That shouldn't dissuade you from learning more, of course. The legendary Wandering Earl has written an excellent book about working on cruise ships that should be considered a must-buy. Elsewhere, check cruiseshipjob.com, allcruisejobs.com, or the cruise ship websites themselves.

- **Electricians** — a classic occupation that won't be disappearing any time soon. While you probably won't earn a full-time income just from the local expat / nomad communities, you might spread the word of your skills while you're in town, or work with locals in some way. Again, be aware of local registrations and requirements and keep a low profile to avoid blowback.
- **Hair stylist / Barber** — cut, color, and style hair to your client's delight. Focus on the styles locals can't do, or just offer a more value-added service that the locals can't offer.
- **Hostel-running** — some hostels will offer you a free place to stay in exchange for a bit of work during the day. This work-to-stay arrangement is a little different at each place, but there's rarely any money changing hands here. There are also real, full-time jobs at hosteljobs.net, hosteltraveljobs.com, workaway.info, and so on.
- **House-sitting** — watch a house, along with an owner's pets, plants, and so on. This has become a common way to find cheap or free accommodation for digital nomads. One catch is that you can't always stay a place you want for as long as you want, and you're typically making your schedule around the available house-sitting opportunities. Among others, hecktictravels.com and thekings.com.au are some nomads that house-sit on a regular basis. *There's more about house-sitting in Step 2.*
- **Make-up artist** — make people look awesome for photoshoots, stage, weddings, etc. Partner with a photographer for an easy win-win.

- **Massage therapy** — offer services in your home or your client's home. You'll want to be licensed or have some significant experience.
- **Photographer** — weddings, performances, maternity, boudoir, or honeymoons are all places to start. Rent a local studio to create some serious works of art, and/or partner with a make-up artist for a great win-win. Alternatively, take stock photos and sell them online.
- **Plumber** — fix problems related to water and sewer pipes. Much like electricians, there are locals to do the job, but language barriers can make finding the right local more difficult.
- **Property management / Airbnb host** — if you own the place but aren't using it, rent it out! Alternatively, if you know the owner of the place, offer your services as a property manager and rent it out on their behalf. Manage the Airbnb listing and calendar, interface with guests, clean or fix the rooms as needed, then send on the owner's cut as necessary. getpaidforyourpad.com is an excellent book and podcast on the subject.
- **Yacht staff** — play your part on a big boat. If you enjoy being on the water or getting paid to travel, and don't mind working on someone else's schedule, this could be for you. A yacht crew can be comprised of many specialties, but some training / experience are required for all of them. The STCW Basic Safety Training course is a legal requirement, and it isn't exactly cheap. Aim for a Steward(ess) to work indoors, a Deckhand for the outdoors work, or an Engineer or Chef / Cook if you have the skills. Whatever position you choose, be aware of the ship's itinerary before applying. yacrew.com and crewfinders.com are just a couple sites to find jobs.

Worksheet #10: What do you want to do to make money?

Date: _____

Find this at becomingadigitalnomad.com/worksheet10. Print a copy and complete offline, or complete online, then print or save.

OK, let's start with a pop quiz. Of the many jobs you just read about, what are some that caught your eye? List a few of them.

_____

Which of these do you prefer as your *primary* role? This helps to narrow down your options.
Consultant   Employee   Entrepreneur   Freelancer

What are you currently paid to do / make / create? (If you're currently unemployed, think back to your most recent job.)

_____

What elements of your current job would you keep / did you like?

_____

Think back to previous jobs / gigs — what responsibilities or experiences did you enjoy?

_____

144

What have you done with your life?

_____

What sort of skills do you have? What have people paid you to do?

_____

Where to find jobs

Digital nomad and remote-work friendly:
- authenticjobs.com — "the leading job board for designers, hackers, and creative pros." Look for the toggle to show remote jobs only.
- angel.co/jobs — "Speak directly to founders and hiring managers." Almost exclusively start-ups and tech companies.
- europeremotely.com — "curated list of remote jobs for workers based in Europe." Head here if you're happy to work on European time.
- flexjobs.com — they "hand-screen and curate every job and company". There is a monthly subscription fee for job-seekers.
- idealist.org — "Idealist is all about connecting idealists — people who want to do good — with opportunities for action and collaboration."
- jobspresso.co — "work remotely from anywhere. Expertly curated remote jobs in tech, marketing, customer support and more." Employers pay for listings.
- landing.jobs — focusing on "digital talent" jobs such as front-end engineers, full-stack developers, and so on.
- outsourcely.com/remoteworker — a broad array of job categories, but watch out for cheapskates. Employers pay for listings.
- remote.co — wide variety of jobs. Has some community features built-in, along with answers to common questions.
- remoteok.io — use filters to quickly narrow down potential listings. Fair number of non-tech listings.
- saywerk.com — "people are not one size fits all, so why is work structured the same for everyone?" Focused on offering women pre-negotiated flexibility in their jobs (and founded by two women), but welcomes men as well. Several ways of defining 'flexible', including remote work, but read descriptions carefully.

- skipthedrive.com — "free service for job seekers, requiring no registration." More of a search engine/aggregator that sends your clicks to other sites.
- startus.cc/jobs — "a professional network connecting you with the European startup community"
- virtualvocations.com — free to see jobs, but requires a monthly fee to reply or see the full job description. Very America-centric, prefers the term 'telecommuting'.
- weworkremotely.com — "We Work Remotely is the best place to find and list jobs that aren't restricted by commutes or a particular geographic area." Only a handful of main categories, mostly programming, 'business exec', and management jobs, rounded out by customer services, marketing, and that classic 'other' category.
- workingnomads.co — "we curate the best digital jobs for those looking to start their telecommuting career." Primarily development, management, and marketing jobs, with a fairly broad (but smaller) curation of other categories.

Where to find work — specifically for freelancers
- cloudpeeps.com — "search and hire talented independent professionals [f]rom our member-driven community of trusted freelancers." Free for employers to place a job, monthly fee for candidates to send proposals.
- dribbble.com/jobs — "Dribbble is where designers get inspired and hired." Almost entirely designer and developer jobs.
- fiverr.com — create a profile, then offer to do or make specific things for as little as $5. Plenty of upselling possible.
- freelancer.com — create a profile for free, then offer to do or make specific things for an hourly or project rate. Freelancers bid on projects created, and can pay extra to highlight their bid.
- guru.com — over three million members. Create a profile, submit a quote to open gigs, and get hired.

- talent.hubstaff.com — create a profile for free, then offer to do or make specific things for an hourly or project rate. Free for employers to post jobs and for applicants to reply to jobs. Watch for cheapskates.
- powertofly.com — "Women Helping Women Elevate Their Careers". Be sure to search specifically for remote position, as 'hybrid' and 'on-site' jobs are available as well.
- toptal.com — "Hire the Top 3% of Freelance Talent". Not for everyone, obviously. Be ready for a thorough confidential screening process that either places you in their 'top 3%' or finds you looking for work elsewhere.
- upwork.com — the 800-pound gorilla of freelance work. Avoid competing on price, since freelancers around the world will work for less. Take their tests to prove your skills, elicit reviews, and send quality proposals. Can take some time to set things up and

Other options
- careerbuilder.com — use keywords like 'telecommute' or 'remote', then filter further from there. Watch for scammy 'work-at-home' positions that require 'paid training' or excessive personal information.
- indeed.com — use keywords like 'telecommute' or 'remote', then filter further from there. Often links to listings on other websites.
- jobbatical.com — "Because your skills matter more than your passport." I always thought a sabbatical was a chance to *not* work, but the offerings here "provide the visa and relocation help you need to take your dream job." Not location *independent* work, but certainly jobs that support travelers.

Volunteering

While volunteering tends not to overlap much with the digital nomad lifestyle, some nomads find a balance between a cause they can get behind and their current work obligations. Volunteering can provide perks such as a free place to live, some free meals, free access to unique experiences, and so on.

Start by asking yourself a few things:
- What are your goals for volunteering? These aren't about *you*, obviously, and volunteering is a great way to give back to a community you care about.
- How many hours a week can you afford to donate? Most volunteer opportunities will require a certain number of hours / shifts per week, which can interfere with your work obligations.
- Where would you be volunteering? Volunteer positions can be found in urban and rural areas and in many countries, though not every opportunity can be found in every location. You may have to choose which one matters more to you — the place or the opportunity.
- How critical is your need for the internet? Many locations will have at least some internet, but areas outside urban centers rarely have great internet. If e-mail is all you need, you can probably handle that with your smartphone if push comes to shove.
- Volunteer jobs should not cost an arm and a leg to get. The more a program costs, the more suspicious I'd be of it unless it's clear where the money goes.

The programs and websites here merely scratch the surface of what you might get into. Google something like 'volunteer in [city]' or [type of volunteer work] in [city / country] to discover even more possibilities. I would strongly suggest sticking with a few sites that work well for you, as any references or positive mentions of your work are likely tied to that platform and aren't typically portable to others.

OK, so what sort of volunteer work do you want to do?
- **Animal welfare** — rehabilitate, train, clean, protect, or otherwise look after animals. goabroad.com, goeco.org, grassrootsvolunteering.org, thegreatprojects.com, and workaway.info are all good places to start.
- **Building work** — build houses, shelters, or other structures to protect people or possessions from the elements. goabroad.com, grassrootsvolunteering.org, and habitat.org are all worth checking out.
- **Design** — find a charity or area that needs a new website. Or a logo. Whatever. Consider a trade between your skills and room / board.
- **Farm work** — help out on farms, organic, small, or otherwise. Head to freevolunteering.net, helpx.net, workaway.info or wwoof.net.
- **Festival / Event staff** — attend festivals or events for free, provided you first help with security, clean-up, parking cars, or the like. Your best bet is to check the websites of the conventions or events you'd most like to attend — if there isn't a volunteer page.
- **Fruit or vegetable picking** — a yummy way to help people, get fit, and even make a bit of money. Not the easiest job, though, physically speaking. Start at fruitfuljobs.com, helpx.net, pickingjobs.com, and wwoof.net.
- **Medicine / Clinical work** — provide medical assistance to people who need it the most. Best for people with a medical background, but some programs can take volunteers with little or no experience. Start at goabroad.com and vsointernational.org.
- **Teach** — while English remains a popular subject, computers, math, science, and other subjects are in high demand. It's a great warm-up to teaching English for money if you have a good experience. freevolunteering.net, goabroad.com, gooverseas.com, grassrootsvolunteering.org, helpx.net, and volunteerhq.org are all worthy places to start.

Some platforms have a wide variety of volunteer opportunities, so dive deeper:
- helpstay.com claims their founder personally checks every project on the site. Charges a yearly membership, and volunteer opportunities may have additional fees that go to the host.
- staydu.com has a color-coded system to show whether you would "stay and help, stay and pay, or stay for free". Lifetime membership required.
- volunteersbase.com is "free and always will be", but naturally accepts donations to keep going. May not be as highly vetted as others due to the free nature, so ask questions before committing.
- volunteerlatinamerica.com — give you one guess about its focus. Projects include NGOs and individual hosts — look carefully at the description to know. Two-year memberships range from £10 to £50, and a higher-level membership looks to offer more personalized guidance.
- workingtraveller.com has a bit of everything around the world, and is free to get started. They charge €10 a year to show references on your profiles once you've completed some work on their site.
- worldpackers.com features an app to show off their offerings beyond their website. It's free to be a member, but does charge trip fees.

One other option worth considering merges volunteering with co-living: Venture with Impact (venturewithimpact.org) offers 4-week 'skills-based volunteering' opportunities at different locations around the world. This upscale program is far from free, but they provide you with work space and high-speed internet while you volunteer.

Should I incorporate my business?

Quick reminder: I am not a lawyer, tax advisor, or corporation-creating professional. Do your own research, talk to qualified professionals, and do what's best for your own unique interests. This is general advice, nothing more.

Incorporating your business gives it some legitimacy, some legal and tax protections, and may be a great idea. I say *may* for a reason, of course — beyond taking a fair bit of time and money to set up, even the experts at flagtheory.com say there is no 'one size fits all' solution, or 'single best' option for incorporation. (If there were, this section would be over by now.) In some cases, it's easier (and/or cheaper or faster) to create a corporation in another country than in your own.

By default, most businesses that nomads start are Sole Proprietorships or General Partnerships (the exact name of the corporate structure depends on the country). How exactly the paperwork is done is up to the country, state, province, or perhaps even the city, county, or township the business is located in. The biggest issues here involve how you're taxed and what happens if you're sued. Because you and your business are essentially the same entity as a sole proprietor, someone suing your business can also (potentially) take everything you own personally.

An LLC (Limited Liability Corporation) is the American version of a private limited company (and again, the exact name of this structure depends on the country). With an LLC / private limited company, you choose who owns what percentage of the business, and your business and personal assets are separated. If someone tries to sue you, they can only go after what the *business* owns, not what the *person* owns.

One surprising fact: just about anyone can create an LLC in the US, and the fees / requirements are the same whether you're a citizen or not. As far as corporations are concerned, however, each state in the US acts like its own little country. Each has its own filing and paperwork requirements, filing fees, and idiosyncrasies when it comes to dealing with other states and countries. There are four states that are consistently recommended:

- **Delaware** — the only state with the Chancery Court, a special court that makes legally binding decisions on business matters. Judges in this court are trained on corporate business matters, and because it's a separate court, cases are less likely to be delayed. (You may never *need* this court, of course, but needing to resolve a legal matter means it takes less time, in theory.) The state also has a reputation for being business-friendly, flexible, and private. Of the *Fortune 500* companies incorporated in the US, 330 of them incorporated in Delaware. No other state has more than 20.
- **Nevada** — you can thank Las Vegas and the gaming industry for this recommendation. Nevada has no business income tax, franchise fees, capital gains tax, state corporation tax, or inheritance tax, *and* you aren't required to file an income tax return. The state also allows shareholders in the business to stay anonymous, and 'single-member' LLC's are allowed. If you want to be a one-person show, you can. The annual fees are higher here than in other states, however, and the allowed anonymity has created a less-than-savory reputation for businesses incorporated here, even when they're squeaky-clean. Reputation, deserved or not, matters to some people.
- **Wyoming** — no personal income tax, no corporate state income tax, no franchise tax, few reporting and disclosure obligations, no state business license required, and a few other perks.
- **South Dakota** — no personal income tax, no corporate state income tax, no capital gains tax, fewer items to file on an ongoing basis, and so on.

Plenty of services exist to work through the paperwork and submit it to the correct offices on your behalf. Expect them to charge you their own processing fees on top of the state fees. Among others, incfile.com, incorporate.com, and myllc.com are three good places to start. Some are state-specific and service-specific, such as the hope-you-remember-it bestwyomingregisteredagent.com (which serves as a local registered agent for you).

No matter where you create a corporation, be aware this isn't a one-and-done process. You'll need to file some paperwork, such as an annual report, on a regular basis. If you plan to do business in other states, you may need to 'foreign qualify' your business in those 'foreign' states. Before filing in a given state, get an idea of how much the paperwork costs to file on a quarterly / annual basis so you can budget for it.

For more advanced or exotic corporate structures, your best bet is to start at a place like incorporations.io, which aims to identify which options are best for you. You'll need to be pretty fluent in the corporate lingo to make the most of this website, so Google any terms that are unfamiliar.

Beyond the USA, Estonia offers an 'e-residency' program (e-resident.gov.ee) that gives non-Estonians access to Estonian services. This program offers no right to actually live in the country (just like owning an LLC in the US offers you no residency rights there), and a background check is run on applicants to ensure you're a decent human being. Once approved, you get a physical 'digital identity card', which lets you 'sign' documents and otherwise prove your e-residency. Since its launch in December 2014, this process has come a long way in a short time, and no longer requires any trips to Estonia. However, you'll need to pick up your digital identity card at some point, of course, so why not take a trip there?

The next step for e-residents (and for some, the primary reason to become an e-resident) might be to open an EU business. Just like in the US, companies exist to make starting a private limited company in Estonia (called *osaühing* or abbreviated as OÜ) easier. One standout is xolo.io (formerly called leapin.eu), an Estonian company that piggybacks on the Estonian e-residency program. (Their blog is a bit self-promotional, but features some good first-person stories of how people are working without borders.) For one monthly fee, paperwork is handled, mail digitized, a local bank account created, a debit card provided, and compliance requirements are met. Beyond Leapin, the Estonian government has an excellent page at e-resident.gov.ee/ run-a-company showing a list of approved service providers, broken up into categories like Banking, Virtual Offices, and so on. Stay up to date on the unofficial but informative Facebook group for Estonian e-residents at facebook.com/groups/eResidents.

As of publication, Estonia is the only country with an e-residency program, and few others appear to be on the horizon. This is very much an emerging concept, however, and as governments realize the benefits of 21st-century governance, other programs may be announced.

Tax stuff

Another quick reminder: This is a large, complex field, and it feels like it only gets messier when you work abroad. I'm not a tax professional, just an author who's done a fair bit of research. Seek advice from a qualified tax professional as appropriate for your tax situation, and do your own due diligence on the resources and ideas mentioned here.

Taxes. Blergh. While they're not the subject people choose to think about when starting a new life, they're a necessary thing to think about. The good news is that there are plenty of tax strategies to minimize how much tax you pay. The bad news is that it can take a fair bit of time to stay compliant with an ever-changing set of rules.

The first big question nomads ask is *where do I pay my taxes?* The simple answer that applies to most people: as few places as possible. Your home country may expect a share of your income (sorry, Americans), but for the most part the countries where you live as a nomad are unlikely to require you to file a formal tax report. Why? Essentially, you're there as a tourist, not as a resident. (This is one of those things that *seriously* changes when you go from the nomad life to the expat life, since the expat life has you doing things from a resident's perspective at times.)

Some thoughts as we get started on this next section:
- Most tax laws and systems around the world simply aren't designed to collect taxes from digital nomads. They're very much stuck in a decades-old way of thinking, which is a shame — but also means they're not usually recognizing a digital nomad as a person they need to collect taxes from.
- As a basic principle, you're more likely to be considered a resident of the country where you've spent 183 days or more during the calendar or tax year.

- There are essentially three types of taxation systems used around the world: citizenship-based taxation (the system used in the USA), residential taxation (used by many developed countries), and territorial taxation (commonly seen in developing countries like Costa Rica and Panama, but also in tax-friendly countries like Singapore and Macau).
- Most countries have signed double-taxation treaties so that you're not double-taxed on the same income. Whichever country calls you a resident (or citizen) is more likely to be where you'll be paying taxes. You may still have to file a tax return or form in multiple countries, but you probably won't be paying income tax in multiple places.
- You'll be paying taxes as you travel whether you like it or not. Most countries feature a Value-Added Tax (VAT), which is already figured into the cost of your product or service. Other countries add sales tax, taxes on your accommodations, excise taxes, taxes on imported stuff and so on. In other words, taxes are already built into the price of things — they're less visible, but they're being paid. Just because you might not pay a formal *income* tax doesn't mean you're able to avoid *all* taxes.
- There's also the concept of the 'tourist tax' to consider — that is, the reality you'll pay more as a tourist than a resident would. You'll likely be shopping at more foreigner-friendly markets instead of the places locals shop. You might be buying imported products instead of what's produced by locals. This is reasonably easy to avoid, *if* you shop, eat, and drink like locals.
- Just as you wouldn't actively avoid trying to pay taxes if you were still living in your country of birth / citizenship, don't try to get away from complying with requirements as a nomad. The chances of the past catching up with you and creating a bureaucratic nightmare only increases the longer you try to get away with it.

Basics for Americans

The bad news: Americans are expected to pay taxes on their income, no matter where in the world they earn it.

The good news: the Foreign Earned Income Exclusion allows you to exclude up to $104,100 of income earned outside the US in 2018. Anything made beyond that, and the IRS will want their share. The exact amount goes up around 1-2% each year.

Any income made from the US can't be excluded, of course, so get your deductions in line. You'll have to have been outside the US for 330 days of the calendar year to qualify for the FEIE, however. You might be able to avoid state income taxes if you set up a virtual office in certain states, such as Florida, but obviously, research this for yourself.

Resources
The IRS' Publication 54 is a Tax Guide for U.S. Citizens and Resident Aliens Abroad. More info at irs.gov/forms-pubs/about-publication-54. Two services (among others) that can help for fees are at greenbacktaxservices.com and onlinetaxman.com.

Basics for Canadians

Becoming a non-resident is one major step to avoiding taxes in Canada. This is not done simply by leaving the country, however — you'll also need to close your bank accounts, cancel your driver's license, sell your home, not have income sources from the country, *and* spend less than 180 days in the country during the calendar year. This is a holistic test, and it's one that also considers the ties you've created with the country you're moving *to*. Giving up your residency doesn't mean giving up your citizenship, of course.

This is not an act to be done lightly. It will take some months of dealing with bureaucracy to get out of the system, and if you decide to become a resident in Canada again, you'll need to set a lot of these things up again. It's also getting harder to set this up, as countries realize this loss of tax revenue is unlikely to be made up later on. Things the government might have let slide in past years may now be considered reasons to deny or challenge your non-residency claim. Nancie McKinnon also suggests, "I came back to Canada this year after being away for 17 years. I would recommend that an accountant be hired to complete your first tax return."

Resources
canada.ca/en/revenue-agency.html
canada.ca/en/revenue-agency/services/tax/international-non-residents/information-been-moved/determining-your-residency-status.html

Basics for Europeans

Europe has a mish-mash of tax laws, but in general, you're taxed where you're listed or registered as a *resident,* not necessarily where you're staying. You should be taxed as the nationals of that country are, meaning you should be able to receive allowances and deductions as the locals do. Since there are hundreds of possible combinations of nationalities and residencies, you'll need to do your own research for your specific case.

Resources
europa.eu/youreurope/citizens/work/taxes/income-taxes-abroad/index_en.htm

Basics for Australians

Australians are expected to declare all of their income to the Australian Tax Office (ATO). Theoretically, you can declare yourself as a non-resident if you can show you'll be living somewhere else for two or more years as a permanent resident. In reality, this is a high bar for digital nomads, which are usually moving around more often than that. For most Australians, it'll be easier to stay a tax resident, then either report your taxes or set up a business.

Resources
ato.gov.au/Individuals/International-tax-for-individuals/Going-overseas/

Basics for New Zealanders

As a resident of New Zealand, you'll pay New Zealand taxes on your worldwide income (although the country will give tax credits to lessen the blow of double taxation, it's not guaranteed). If you spend more than 325 days in any 12-month period (not necessarily a calendar or tax year), and don't have an enduring relationship with the country, you're considered a non-resident for tax purposes. Non-residents only need to pay New Zealand tax on income from New Zealand sources.

The rules here can be pretty tricky, but the official sources emphasize that if you have a "permanent place of abode" in New Zealand, you'll always be considered a tax resident regardless of where you live.

Resources
ird.govt.nz/international/residency/personal
ird.govt.nz/forms-guides/number/forms-200-299/ir292-guide-nz-tax-residence.html

What if I'm not a resident *anywhere*?

If you're moving every few months and not spending more than 6 months in a given country, it's unlikely any government would be able to request and collect income taxes from a non-resident like you. Again, this is one of those situations where laws and rules just haven't caught up with this 21st century lifestyle — and again, you're still paying tax in some form everywhere you go. You're just not submitting or filing a formal income tax return to the countries you're temporarily staying in, since you're there on a tourist visa. (You may have attained some sort of taxable status if you have a work, retirement, education, or other type of visa, even if you're not formally considered a resident — again, do your own research for the type of visa and country in question and consult with licensed help as appropriate.)

If you're still considered a resident of your home country, even if you haven't lived there in years, consider that the place to file. The country your business is incorporated in may require some formal business filings — do some research or talk to the person that set things up for you to understand what's required. Again, you may not have to *pay* anything, but you still need to *file* the formal paperwork stating your income and exemptions.

Moving and accessing money

Now that we've committed to paying our taxes (or at least complying with tax requirements), it's time to address another headache. We're *way* past traveler's checks / cheques and personal checks in the 21st century, and carrying any significant amount of cash is a risk travelers don't need to take. For most travelers, having a few debit / credit cards to access cash and / or pay for things is all you need. The exact process will look and work differently for you based on your nationality and where you're going, naturally.

The good news: it's easier than ever to move money around the world.

The bad news: it does require some setup, there are some fees to pay attention to, and it can be a pain to replace the cards if they get lost or stolen.

Start with a bank account

A traditional bank account in your home country isn't what nomads may think of as a first choice, but consider it an important lifeline to set up before leaving your home country. It's a classic option that's at least a fallback option depending on how other things might work. If you already have a bank account in your home country, it's time to see how much you're paying in monthly fees or charges. Look through your bank statements (electronic or paper) with a fine-toothed comb to find out, then figure out whether it's the right account for you. I'd personally be opening an account at a bank that doesn't charge me money for the privilege of holding my money or making money off of my money.

Whether you decide to open a new account or continue with the account you already have, there are some important housekeeping things to do with your account:
- Cancel any services or add-ons you're not using.
- Set up electronic bank statements and turn off paper statements. The less paper mail that's coming to your soon-to-be-former doorstep, the better. Already on electronic statements? Great!
- Overdrafts should be avoided at all costs — and a 2010 US law prohibits American banks from processing a transaction if the account has insufficient funds by default. You can opt *in* to this coverage, and a bank will make it easy to do that since it'll let them charge you for overdrafts. It will be harder to opt *out*, but there's always a way. Don't opt in to start so you don't have to find out.
- Call or visit your local bank branch. Let them know you'll be traveling to [insert country here], and that you're leaving on

[insert date here]. Banks have an array of security systems for fraud prevention, and suddenly spending hundreds of dollars in a country halfway around the world can set off alarm bells that can freeze your account or even cancel your card.
- Request an updated debit card. By now, just about every bank in the world should be issuing debit cards with a 'chip' on them. More properly called an EMV chip (Europay Mastercard and Visa, the companies that developed it), the 'chip and PIN' combo is more secure than the magnetic stripe on the back of the card. Bonus points if it has a 'tap-to-pay' or RFID technology, although those technologies aren't usable everywhere. This usually needs to be mailed to you, so try to do this at least 2 weeks before leaving.
    - ***I already have a debit card with a chip!*** Great! When does it expire? If it'll expire within the next 12 months, get the new one now to save issues about receiving it (very few banks will ship debit cards overseas). Don't worry about it if the card's expiration date is more than a year away, or if you're only trying out the nomadic lifestyle.
- If you want your traveling partner to have access to this bank account, request a duplicate or additional card.
- Make some paper reference cards with your account's details on them. Put them with your other important paperwork.
- Know your ATM withdrawal limit per transaction or per day. Remember your bank will add its own fees and convert the requested currency from your home currency. Either of those things can put your request over that withdrawal limit and deny a transaction.
- Tear up any paper checks / cheques attached to your account. Seriously. Shred them if you can. In over ten years of living abroad, I have never once needed a paper check. Save one to show your routing and account numbers, or write them down and keep them in a safe space.
- If you'll be receiving checks, see if your bank has an app that allows you to deposit them via the app. If they do,

download it. Note these apps will usually only work with the original check, not a picture or scan of it.

Add a Paypal account

Available in over 200 countries, Paypal (paypal.com) is the most well-known ways of moving money from one person or small business to another without a bank account. I think of my Paypal account as my primary way of collecting money, since I've had it for well over a decade at this point. The service isn't perfect, and has been known to occasionally lock people's money up for security or verification issues, but remains a widely-used service for lots of people.

The person that's paying you only needs your e-mail address and a credit or debit card. Once received, the balance can be re-spent anywhere Paypal is accepted, sent to a bank account, or cashed out via the Paypal debit card (currently only available to American and British residents). Do not confuse this with the expensive prepaid offering — the debit card I'm talking about here deducts money from your Paypal balance (and if necessary, your bank or backup source).

I wish the service would be more understanding of the digital nomad lifestyle. Still, as of late 2019, it's still the largest and best-known service of its kind, so that means our best option is to work with its idiosyncrasies. Here are some tips.

- If you're an American, get the Paypal debit card. I'd highly recommend starting this process at least six weeks before you leave, since it can take some time to confirm your address and receive the card. Once you have it, Paypal's debit card can get cash at virtually any ATM in the world.
- One annoying part of Paypal is their casual rejection of transactions from 'new' countries. The best way to proactively deal with this is to give their Customer Service line a call and to update your Travel Profile. You can also login on paypal.com, then click Profile > My Settings > Travel Plans, or try going directly to paypal.com/businessprofile/mysettings/travelplan/add. If

you forget, give them a call if your card is blocked, then unblock it and update your Travel Profile.
- When calling Customer Service, one great way to speed things up is to log onto through the site to get a one-time passcode. Click 'Contact' at the bottom of the page, click 'Contact Customer Service', then click 'Call us'. The next page will show you a six-digit one-time password that expires one hour after it is first shown, so get that call started! While this won't guarantee a free pass through *all* the security questions, it's a great shortcut.
- If at all possible, stay logged into your Paypal account during your call. In some cases, you might be asked for transaction data, or (if declined at an ATM) you might be asked how much money you were trying to withdraw. Convert it in your head and give your answer in US dollars. You might also be asked if you can receive a text message — if you can, they'll send a confirmation number that way.
- Customer service is not open 24 / 7. Officially, hours are Monday-Friday from 5am-10pm Pacific time and Saturday-Sunday 6am-8pm Pacific time. Anecdotally speaking, the best time to call in with an issue is right when it opens (start your call just **after** the hour to avoid the 'our offices are currently closed' message).
- I haven't seen many people use the Paypal.me service, which is a super-easy way to get paid. In essence, you can set up a short username (it'll look like paypal.me/YOURUSERNAMEHERE) that becomes a super-easy link to get people paying you.
    - Want to specify an amount? Add a number — send someone to paypal.me/YOURUSERNAMEHERE/100 to ask for $100 US dollars (the default currency). You can customize the currency by adding the standard three-letter code after the number (for example: paypal.me/YOURUSERNAMEHERE/100eur will ask for 100 Euros).
    - The catch: a paypal.me page can only show one name / logo — if you have more than one business, you'll need to set this up on different accounts.

Consider a credit card

Whether used for making payments or needed to make a guarantee or deposit, a credit card is a common tool in people's wallets. There are a ton of different types of cards out there, complete with a dizzying array of rewards, options, and fees. Covering this industry would be a full-time job in itself, mainly since programs seem to change unannounced or at the drop of a hat. I'll refrain from recommending any specific credit card providers, but I *will* recommend you be cautious of any sites that try to compare credit cards for you. Too often, the affiliate links they use give them an incentive to promote some links and bury others. I don't know about you, but this is not my idea of 'neutral' advice.

Pay attention to how many points or miles certain actions will give you, along with the interest rates at play. Make it a point to read the terms and conditions to ensure you understand what's happening.

One pro-tip before leaving: Freeze your credit — this action prohibits companies from accessing your credit file, and makes it harder for anyone to open a line of credit in your name. This 'credit freeze' or 'security freeze' needs to be done with each of the three credit agencies (Experian, Equifax, and TransUnion) As of September 2018, these credit freezes are now free, and as of publication, the URL's to visit are:

- Equifax: equifax.com/personal/credit-report-services/ (or call 1-800-685-1111)
- Experian: experian.com/freeze/center.html (or call 1-888-397-3742)
- TransUnion: transunion.com/credit-freeze (or use the myTransUnion app)

Other options for Americans

A debit card from Charles Schwab reimburses ATM fees. This checking account is linked to a no-monthly-fee brokerage account. Apply while still in the US — if you're not, you might have some luck using a VPN. Get started at content.schwab.com/web/retail/public/get-started/checking/

A debit card from Fidelity also reimburses ATM fees (but not their 1% foreign transaction fee). Learn more at fidelity.com/cash-management/atm-debit-card.

Venmo

As their website (venmo.com) says. "Paying your friends back for pizza shouldn't cost more than your slice." It's a service of Paypal, and is a fine way of sending or receiving payments for smaller or casual uses. Sending money using your Venmo balance, bank account, or debit card is free, and receiving money from authorized businesses is free as well. This is a mobile app first and payment platform second. I haven't seen or heard of this much outside of the US, however.

As of June 2018, Venmo launched a physical debit card. As of publication it's only available in the US and *only works in the US*, so it's borderline useless to nomads. I mention it here in the hopes that it becomes more useful, and for the digital nomads traveling to the US.

Zelle

Zelle (zellepay.com) is the big banks' response to Venmo, Square Cash, and other payment apps. It's "backed by the nation's leading banks and credit unions," according to their website, and you can transfer money from your bank account to someone else's in a matter of minutes. Not every bank is part of the network, but it'll still work so long as your bank debit card is registered.

While Zelle doesn't charge any fees for using your service, your bank might charge for deposits or withdrawals. Zelle saves a step in you having to add cash to your balance (or cashing out), but they only recommend doing business with people you are familiar with, since it doesn't seem like there's any ability to refund transactions. The person you're doing business must have an American bank account, since that's where they'll be receiving the money, but they don't have to have Zelle.

Other options for Europeans

N26

N26 (n26.com) is Europe's first mobile / online bank. Founded in Berlin in 2013, their debit card pairs perfectly with their app to do everything from getting cash out of ATMs to transferring money to friends. Fees are low, and the no-monthly-fee account can handle plenty of stuff. Their MoneyBeam technology covers transfers to/from anyone, whether they're another N26 customer or not. The N26 Black card (at €5.90 / month) offers fee-free ATM transactions, worldwide travel insurance, and more. Until recently, you had to be a resident of Europe, but now it's working in more countries than ever before.

Revolut

With offerings very similar to N26, you'd be forgiven for thinking Revolut (revolut.com) was a clone of N26. The app works with the debit card, and the basic service is free, while the Premium service is £7 and 'Metal' service (which adds a concierge service) £13 a month. Your account also includes an IBAN and current account in the UK — and a chance to buy some cryptocurrency if you're so inclined.

Monzo

Monzo (monzo.com) is another 'bank-in-an-app' offering with debit cards available, but is only available to UK residents as of publication. Launched in late 2015, and today's members have a current account, sort code, and other traditional banking features alongside a 21st-century interface.

Other options for almost everyone

Monese

Offering a UK current account without a UK address or credit history, Monese (monese.com) helps get around some of the catch-22's if starting out in the UK. A starter account is free to open, but charges higher fees for ATM withdrawals and currency exchanges (upgrade to the 'Classic' account at £5 / month to get a free debit card and free ATM withdrawals, or the Premium account at £15 / month for freebies while traveling).

Paysera

Paysera (paysera.com) is available in 180 countries and in 30 currencies. Their service includes a debit card to withdraw cash, the ability to have a checkout on your website, an IBAN number, and gives you the ability to make payments on Europe's SEPA system. While the fees are low, they will vary according to the country and bank.

Payoneer

Think of Payoneer (payoneer.com) as the 'Paypal / debit card for everyone else'. It's not *quite* the international version of Paypal, but their 'Payoneer Mastercard' is available to people around the world. They have an impressive list of partnerships with companies you may work with as a digital nomad, including Upwork, Fiverr, CJ Affiliate, ClickBank, Rakuten,

Teespring, Airbnb, Getty Images, 99designs, Envato, and PeoplePerHour. Just like the Paypal card, you can withdraw cash from ATMs or deposit your earnings in your bank account. Better still, your clients can pay you via Payoneer using an e-check, local bank transfer, or debit/credit card.

Transferwise

One of Transferwise's (transferwise.com) premier services is the ability to send money at the 'real exchange rate', also known as the mid-market rate. Clients can send you money via ACH (Automated Clearing House) payments, with much lower fees for payments made within their 'borderless' accounts. Debit cards are available, and they currently operate in almost 60 countries and offer over 500 'currency routes'. If you're moving money from one currency to another or accepting lots of payments in different currencies, they can definitely save you money.

Cryptocurrencies

If you've ever heard of Bitcoin, Ethereum, Litecoin, or any other cryptocurrencies, you might have wondered if these can be spent in everyday life. Cryptocurrencies are electronic currencies created by individuals or companies (not by countries) with the security and transactions handled by cryptography. A single coin may be worth anywhere from thousands of US dollars to a tiny fraction of a cent. Cryptocurrencies are considered high-risk investments (even by its supporters) or gambling (often by its detractors).

With that said, the decentralized nature of these currencies makes them very difficult to be shut down by the governments of the world. A transaction between two people can happen — without the need of a bank or any other central authority — quickly, safely, and for a fraction of the costs imposed by banks.

Can you actually use cryptocurrencies in real life? Yes, definitely. More and more sites allow you to pay using cryptocurrencies, and there are start-ups offering debit cards connected to your cryptocurrency accounts. Few companies in this industry are mature or stable enough to recommend quite yet, but do your own research and keep your ears to the ground.

Since information about cryptocurrencies changes at a moment's notice, here are a few sites to stay up to date:
- coinmarketcap.com — shows market caps, prices, the exchanges where each coin can be bought, and the sales volume for virtually the entire industry.
- coindesk.com — a great news source for all things related to cryptocurrency.
- themerkle.com — another great cryptocurrency news source.
- cryptopanic.com — a news aggregator that combines news from Reddit and websites, while showing prices of top coins all on one screen.
- airdropalert.com — ready to get some cryptocurrency for free? Airdrops are run by the makers of coins to get people talking about them on social media. There's some technical stuff to set up to get started, but it's a good cryptocurrency learning experience that won't require you to spend any money.

Most people start by converting some fiat currency to cryptocurrency, and a few exchanges are set up to offer that. Be aware that some credit card companies will not allow you to purchase cryptocurrency, so use a debit card or a bank account instead:
- coinbase.com — pay by bank wire, debit card, or credit card (with lower fees but longer wait time if purchased by bank wire). Also look at Coinbase Pro and see how their fees compare.
- gemini.com — started by the Winklevoss twins of Facebook fame. There aren't as many cryptocurrencies to buy here (Bitcoin, Ethereum, ZCash, and Litecoin only),

but Gemini still serves as a good 'on-ramp'. They're regarded as one of the most compliant exchanges around, and are available to residents of most states in the US, Canada, Hong Kong, Singapore, South Korea and the U.K.
- kraken.com — established in 2011, Kraken is a partner in the world's first cryptocurrency bank, Fidor Bank AG. Europeans can deposit funds via SEPA for free, while Americans, Canadians, and Japanese can send bank wire deposits for free. Once your fiat has been converted, buy over a dozen cryptocurrencies on their exchange.
- bitstamp.net — established in 2011, this exchange lets you trade Euros, US dollars, and a handful of cryptocurrencies. It's considered one of the best exchanges for Europeans, but also for credit card holders in dozens of other countries since you can purchase bitcoin via credit / debit card from almost 90 countries.

I do not recommend Coinmama, Changelly, or LocalBitcoin, as they come with higher fees and poorer exchange rates. I *do* recommend several other crypto exchanges a couple of paragraphs further on, though.

Security will be tight when registering and logging in, as it should be. Expect to complete some verification procedures, which may include uploading a picture of your ID, a copy of your bank statement, or a selfie of you holding your ID. Two-factor authentication (also known as 2FA) is a way to further secure your account, so set that up where possible as well. As additional security, withdraw your coins from the exchange and store them in your 'wallet' — either a software wallet (e.g. a program/app for your computer) or a hardware wallet (e.g. a physical device the size of a USB drive) will work. Storing coins on exchanges exposes you to the risk of them being hacked, so transfer them to your wallet if you're not actively trading them.

Once you've bought some Bitcoin (or Ethereum or Litecoin), you can transfer it to any number of other crypto-only exchanges like Bibox, Binance, Bittrex, Gate.io, or Kucoin. Each exchange offers different cryptocurrencies for sale, but the most popular coins are available almost everywhere. Bear in mind that there are almost always fees to withdraw your coins, and they'll vary dramatically based on the exchange and the coin.

As 'crypto debit cards' go, there are a few options:
- Bitpay debit card (US residents only) - bitpay.com/card
- Cryptopay (available worldwide) - cryptopay.me
- Wirex debit card (EEA, or European Economic Area) - wirexapp.com/card

Each of these companies has a fee schedule, of course.

Wrapping it all up

Make no mistake — despite all this talk about moving money around the internet, cash remains king in many parts of the world. It's still the simplest way to pay for things in the physical world and offers the best chance of getting discounts on larger purchases.
Use your cards to get cash, and know that it's generally better to make fewer withdrawals in larger amounts.

Step 4: get affairs in order

I will start this section by apologizing for the name of this step — it can easily sound like you're preparing for an upcoming death. This is as far from death as you can get, though in a sense we are talking about transitioning from one life to another. That means getting things set up for your new life.

The first big question to ask: **How much lead time will you need?** Even if you're just trying the lifestyle out as a test, there's a lot of logistical stuff to consider, and lots of pieces to the puzzle here. Getting (or renewing) your passport, buying your plane ticket, tying up any loose ends, working out bank and other financial arrangements, and other considerations unique to you and your personal situation.

What sort of time frame are we talking about between deciding you're going to become (or test being) a digital nomad, and actually leaving?

- **As an absolute minimum: 1 week.** This assumes you already have a passport and a location picked out. You're giving away most of your stuff, selling very little, can move out at will, and are unemployed, don't have to give notice to quit your job, or are taking your work with you.
- **As a practical minimum: 3-4 weeks.** This assumes you've already started the process for your passport, have some stuff to sell or give away, and need to give some notice before you can move out or quit your job.
- **As a good target: 2-3 months.** This assumes you need to start the process to get your passport, have quite a bit of stuff to sell or store, or need more time to move out or quit your job.

It goes without saying that these aren't fixed timeframes, and that every situation is unique. Selling a car or a house (especially in a down market) can take months, and you can't really leave until all that business is taken care of.

Your anchor

No, we're not talking about the heavy thing on a ship. For digital nomads, think of an anchor as a person still in your home country or city who will receive mail, store stuff for you, tie up any loose ends, and so on. You may also want to entrust them with power of attorney, although nomads rarely need to do this. Your anchor can be a close friend, a trusted family member, or a friendly neighbor. They're less necessary if you're just trying the nomad lifestyle as a test, but it's helpful to identify someone that would do it, in case you decide to go ahead. While an anchor is not a required thing to have, they can help in plenty of ways.

Your anchor doesn't have to be a person. If there's no one you trust to handle things like this, you can hire a mail-receiving service. These services offer monthly plans to receive mail, scan mail, forward mail, deposit checks into your account, recycle or trash junk mail, and so on.

Here are a few mail-receiving services to look into. Keep in mind that most of these, but not all, receive the mail at a US address, and international forwarding fees will apply.
- **Earth Class Mail** is one of the original businesses in the industry. Their packages start at $69 a month, and are best for businesses where the owner is nomadic but needs a prestigious-looking address. Check depositing is part of some packages, and is available for an additional fee in others. Learn more at earthclassmail.com.
- **Clevver Mail** is a cheaper option for receiving and scanning mail at 40 locations around the world, but doesn't offer any check-depositing options. Monthly pricing depends on which address you want to use, but start around €6 a month. Also offers phone numbers, phone forwarding services, and incorporation services. Learn more at clevvermail.com.

- **Traveling Mailbox** offers plenty of scanning and up to three mailbox recipients on its most basic plan ($15 / month). They also offer a 'SCANpak', which lets you mail in your paper receipts for them to scan and upload to your online mailbox. Check cashing is available for an additional fee. Learn more at travelingmailbox.com.
- **Virtual Post Mail** offers several packages starting at $15 a month, based on how much mail needs processing. An unlimited service starts at $30 a month, and check cashing is available for an additional fee. Learn more at virtualpostmail.com.
- **Mailbox Forwarding** offers up to 15 items scanned in the basic plan of $15 a month. One additional feature is a (shared) toll-free fax line, and any faxes received count as a scanned item. Learn more at mailboxforwarding.com.
- **Scan My Post** is a UK-based version of the same service, starting at £4.99 a month for 10 scans. Depositing cheques is available for an additional fee. Learn more at scanmypost.co.uk.

Whether you have an anchor or use a forwarding service, aim to reduce the paper you need to receive as you travel to the smallest possible amount.

All about that (home)base

If you own your home or have a long-term lease and you have reason to return there frequently, your homebase can quickly become an important part of your digital nomad life. Beyond the obvious potential revenue source (rent it out on Airbnb when you're not using it, if allowed, for example), it remains the place to store your extra stuff, keep your extra or formal clothing, and call home. If you choose to be a 'part-time nomad' for some months of the year, you'll always have the space to return to when you're done traveling. The biggest disadvantage is that it's a constant expense, even if it isn't earning any income. Consider hiring someone local to maintain the place while you're away.

Having a homebase only makes sense if you'll actually *use* it, of course. Some folks will think of a homebase as a *city* they return to, not a specific house or apartment. However you think of a homebase, know what you'll do with the space before leaving. Things are so much easier to set up that way.

Some other loose ends to tie up before leaving

Reduce the amount of paper being sent to your soon-to-be-former address. Part of this is to ensure you receive important information, but part of it is also to avoid identity theft. The ideal amount of paper you'd have to receive would be zero, but that's virtually impossible, so aim for as little as you can. Another theme here rests on the assumption that you're leaving one life behind and starting another — if this is not the case, some items on this list won't be needed.

- Setup / create paperless / electronic banking — contact your bank or log onto their website and switch to paperless / electronic banking.
- Setup paperless / electronic credit card statements — contact your credit card company or log onto their website and switch to paperless / electronic banking.
- Setup a Paypal account, if you didn't during the last step. If you've never heard of Paypal, think of it as an online bank with no branches. You can send or receive money directly from their website, and you can spend that money in lots of places. Aim to get everything as 'authorized' as possible. If you're eligible for the Paypal debit card, get it.
- Setup a Dropbox account. If you've never heard of Dropbox, it's an easy way to backup your files on a secure server. Download their app to your computer / tablet / phone. On a desktop, it'll look like a standard file explorer window, but everything inside that folder is backed up on Dropbox's servers.
- Sell your car or end your car's lease.

- Electric, water, and internet services — cancel them or put the services in someone else's name. Call, e-mail, or write as appropriate.
- Cancel newspaper and magazine subscriptions — call, e-mail, or write as appropriate.
- Want to throw a going away party? It's a great chance to get together with your friends or family one last time before heading out, to answer people's questions about your journey, and so on.
- Any ongoing or lingering work obligations? Get your last paycheck, turn in any materials, help train your replacement, etc.
- If you're a pet owner, what will you do with your pets? Some nomads will travel with their furry friends — remember to research what treatments are needed for them to enter a country, and keep their paperwork in order. Some nomads will take their animals with them on a temporary basis, but the reality is that providing a 'forever home' is much more difficult with the nomad lifestyle. If you're just testing the lifestyle out, who can your pet stay with for those days / weeks?
- Unlock your smartphone, if it's not already — if you bought your phone through a carrier at a subsidized rate, it may be 'locked' to only accept that carrier's brand of SIM card. (If you've had more than one working SIM card in the same phone, it's almost certainly unlocked.) Each company, and some countries, has different rules about how to do this if it's needed. (Don't have a smartphone yet? Pick one up! It's one of the most versatile tools out there.)
- Add Whatsapp, Viber, Google Maps, Currency and maybe even Tinder to your phone. Whatsapp is the world's most popular messenger service outside the US and China, while Viber offers great rates on phone calls. Google Maps is the industry standard, and the Currency app is a must-have to show current exchange rates and show the last-updated rates while offline. Tinder has many more uses beyond its reputation as a hookup app — be clear what you're looking for in your profile, of course.

- Another app to consider adding to your phone is called NotOK. Once open, one tap sends a message to your trusted contacts with GPS coordinates of your exact location. Your friend or family can then contact you, a mutual friend, or the local authorities. There are other apps that send a message to people you choose, but I like the one-tap simplicity of this one. More info at notokapp.com.

Let's not forget about our health before leaving.
- Whatever type of health insurance your company or country offers, get a routine dental check-up done. If they recommend more work, there's a very good chance you can get that work done cheaper where you're going — even without insurance. This is especially true if you're going to Southeast Asia or Eastern Europe.
- Being up-to-date with your country's recommended schedule of vaccinations is always a good idea. The US CDC has guides for kids (cdc.gov/vaccines/schedules/hcp/imz/child-adolescent.html) and adults (cdc.gov/vaccines/schedules/hcp/imz/adult.html). In some countries it'll be easy and cheap to get them, but it's just another thing to do once you're there.
- Few vaccinations are specifically required for travel, but when they're required, it's usually for a good reason. Go to cdc.gov/travel, choose where you're going, and select any of the boxes that apply to get a list of which vaccinations are necessary.
- Whatever vaccinations you get, keep the paperwork with your passport. Jennifer Booker Smith notes, "In Africa, we had to show proof of vaccination to board any flights to yellow fever zones, for example."

What about medicines?

Do some research on any medications you're regularly taking, based on where you're going. There are a few plausible scenarios to keep in mind:
- The brand names you're used to may not be available where you're going. Ask an American pharmacist for Panadol and you'll likely get a blank look. Ask almost any pharmacist around the world for paracetamol (the active ingredient in brand-name medicines like Tylenol or Panadol) and they'll point you in the right direction. *In other words: look up the active ingredient of what you're taking and write it down. That'll likely be easier than trying to pronounce it in many cases, anyway!*
- The medications you need may be cheaper and of the same quality where you're going. Also, medicines that might be considered prescriptions where you are now can be bought over-the-counter in other countries. *In other words: no need to stock up before you leave.*
- The medications you need may be difficult to find, more expensive, or of a lower quality / dosage. My wife notes, "very few Korean pharmacies actually stock insulin." *In other words: stock up before you leave.*
- Note some countries (such as Thailand, Japan, Egypt, and other Arab countries) restrict certain medicines from entering their countries, **even if it's a legitimate prescription in your home country**. Your now-illegal medicine may earn you a fine or even detention. Keep medicines in their original containers, and have a doctor's letter detailing what you're taking. *In other words: do your research to avoid potentially ruining your trip.*
  - For more about traveling with medicine into Thailand, see thaiembassy.se/en/tourism/restricted-medicine. They're mostly concerned with narcotics and psychotropics.
  - For more about traveling with medicine into Japan, see jp.usembassy.gov/u-s-citizen-services/doctors/importing-medication. They're mostly concerned with

stimulants (such as pseudoephedrine. Adderall, etc.), syringes, and CPAP machines (Continuous Positive Airway Pressure — a device usually used by people to reduce snoring).
  - Regarding Egypt: "An official letter from your GP is required, specifying that the medication you are taking to Egypt is for your personal use only, the quantity you will be carrying and details of your condition. Please note that any medication containing Methadone is NOT permitted into Egypt." (Source: egyptianconsulate.co.uk/FAQ.php#26)
- **Pro-tip:** after you arrive, keep the box of any over-the-counter medications you might buy. Your goal here is to show the pharmacist the box of what worked (if it did), or to try something else the next time (if it didn't).

Let's talk about sex, just for a second.
- Unless you plan to remain celibate during your trip, stock up on your preferred brands of condoms and lubrication. Lube should be tightly wrapped in a resealable bag to avoid the cap opening, and probably belongs in your checked bag. Don't go overboard here — one tube of lube and a large box of condoms is plenty for most people for quite awhile.
- Sex toys sometimes have this annoying habit of vibrating, rotating, or otherwise turning on just as you get to airport security. Whether you choose to put your toys in your carry-on or your checked bag, take the batteries out first to save yourself some potential embarrassment.
- If you're on a birth control pill, the availability, variety, and quality of birth control pills can vary dramatically as you travel the world. Plenty of countries make it easy to get what you need, but stock up ahead of time if you absolutely must have a specific brand, or do some research to see if generic equivalents are a fit as well. "Pharmacists will usually be able to tell you what's approximately equivalent," according to my wife.

Stay connected by voice

One great thing about e-mail is that it just works anywhere in the world. If you need to speak to someone, however, voice / phone calls are country-based, and international calls usually cost much more than local calls. You'll get a local number when you pop in a local SIM card, but you might prefer to have a phone number in your home country as well. (If you plan on making calls, make sure you pick up a plan that allows them — some people pick a 'data-only' plan then get surprised when it doesn't come with minutes). Start at prepaid-data-sim-card.fandom.com/, then navigate to the country you're visiting, but bear in mind details can change. Use this as a baseline, not an always-perfectly-updated tool.

Beyond the local SIM card options, there are plenty of other ways to connect via voice:

- **Skype** (skype.com) is one of the most well-known options for video conferencing, but naturally can handle voice calls as well. Calls from one Skype user to another are always free, and calls that go to a phone (landline or mobile) are quite cheap. If you want a phone number in your home country that will ring through to your Skype (and allow the people calling you to save money), these are available from Skype for a small monthly fee. As of publication, it doesn't appear possible to port an existing mobile phone number to a Skype number.
- **Toll Free Forwarding** (tollfreeforwarding.com) is a perfect way to get a phone number in one of dozens of countries for a monthly fee. Toll-free numbers are great for that professional look, and they also offer PBX (voice menu) services.
- **JustCall** (justcall.io) offers phone numbers in 58 countries, along with a service that records incoming calls. Works with their website, your phone, or apps for your smartphone.

- **Burner** (burnerapp.com) and **Hushed** (hushed.com) are smartphone apps offering a US or Canada phone number that you can 'burn', or dispose of at will, for privacy purposes. These services have monthly fees which include a number of messages or minutes.
- **Google Voice** (voice.google.com) is free, but has to be set up in the US with a US phone number (though there are ways around that).

Wait! I need to keep my number from my home country! If it's a toll-free number, see if your current service provider can forward calls to your new mobile phone number. If they're unable to do that, you may want to consider changing services. There's likely to be a monthly service fee to forward those calls to an international number, and this may be an acceptable cost of doing business.

If it's a mobile number you want to keep, be aware that you'll most likely want to change services as well, unless you want to keep an active service you're barely using. For post-paid plans in some countries, that service might be $40-$50 a month *just* to keep the service active. Most countries will let you port your number from one service provider to another, but this only applies within your country.

Two options to port your American or Canadian number to another service include tossabledigits.com and ting.com. (For other countries, check out voip.ms or plivo.com.) Each company offers options to park your number (but still get SMS and phone calls from it) or forward any calls from it to your local number for a monthly fee. Voice mail, call recording, and other specialized features may also be available.

Paperwork

Make sure all your important paperwork is in one place — a good thing to do, no matter your lifestyle. Pick up a durable plastic A4 / Letter-size folder at your nearest office supply store (ideally something that's water-resistant, or even better, waterproof) and put the following stuff in it:
- Health paperwork
- Tax statements or returns
- Government paperwork (birth certificates, social security, wedding certificate, medical insurance cards)
- Anything that shows property or asset ownership
- Anything else you might put in a safe or safe deposit box

Since this is the 21st century, a scanned backup of these documents on a Dropbox folder or a USB stick is also a good idea. Keep this in a safe place alongside your computer and other electronics.

In-case-of-emergency letters

For those traveling with your spouse or significant other, you may need access to their computer, smartphone, or bank accounts in case of emergency. Since you can't count on them being able to remember every password or share it on command, an in-case-of-emergency letter is an alternative. These are essentially a couple sheets of paper with your most important passwords, bank account information, and so on. This is obviously very sensitive information, so seal the envelope and keep it in with your other paperwork, or give it to your partner for safekeeping in their paperwork. Remember to update this once in awhile — once or twice a year is fine.

Wills

It might sound a bit morbid, but you might also consider making out a will as part of this process. A will's most basic job is to allow you legally-recognized control on how your property is to be distributed, as opposed to the default laws of the state / country. Should you have primary or joint custody of any minors, your will can also state whom you choose to become their guardian(s).

- **Americans:** LegalZoom offers a $89 package (legalzoom.com), and doyourownwill.com offers a 100% free service.
- **Australians:** See freewillsonline.com.au (free) and onlinewillcentre.com.au ($20 AUD) for two of the easiest and cheapest options.
- **Brits:** See makeawillonline.co.uk (£29.50) or tenminutewill.co.uk (£19.99).
- **Canadians:** legalwills.ca ($40 CAD) and formalwill.ca ($59 CAD) are two of the easiest and cheapest options.
- **Europeans:** legal traditions and cultural idiosyncrasies make generalizing very difficult, and I did not discover many 'make-your-will-online services' for Europe. If you have a significant amount of property or assets to your name, consider talking to the appropriate professionals (such as a lawyer, a notary public, and so on) as necessary before leaving your home country.
- **Kiwis:** check out do-it-yourself-wills.co.nz ($30 NZD) and justly.co.nz ($39 NZD).

Learning the local language

If you'll be in the country for more than a week or so, aim to learn at least some of the local language. Expats will use more of the local language, but nomads will find even a few basic phrases and sayings handy.

- duolingo.com — vocabulary and sentence lessons for dozens of languages around the world. Sure, I love the Klingon course as much as anyone else — while not exactly practical, it gives you an understanding of their style. Their free offerings work on your smartphone, tablet, or computer.
- languagedrops.com — more like quick games than worksheets, they have a free app for iOS or Android.
- memrise.com — gamify language learning on your phone or tablet. Free and pro offerings available.
- mosalingua.com — offers a more science-based approach with its own distinctive learning method. Free offerings for phones, tablets, and computers.

Travel insurance

Consider getting travel insurance (also called 'cover' by some companies) before leaving — it's easier that way, though some insurers will sell you a policy after you've left. Several warnings / disclaimers first:

- The world of insurance is complex and confusing, and your needs will be unique. Compare and contrast costs, benefits, and limits of coverage for yourself. Each company has their own rules for which pre-existing conditions are excluded, coverage limits on electronics, upper age limit, length of policy, etc.
- There are any number of aggregators offering to help you compare insurance products and plans. I've opted not to mention them here because sites like these may rank the plans based on how much advertising money they offer or

- how lucrative their affiliate links are. Instead, I've chosen to link directly to the companies themselves so you can make your own comparisons.
- As you're researching, learn whether an insurance company pays the hospital / doctor directly. If they're not, and if all bills have to be paid upfront by yours truly, you're paying out-of-pocket, then working with the insurance company to get reimbursed.
- Travel insurance may exclude the USA because of the high cost of treatment there when compared with the rest of the world, and may also exclude other countries where healthcare costs are high. Double-check the details to ensure the countries you're planning to visit aren't excluded.
- Americans, be aware few companies cover you while you're in the USA. Travelers insurance usually implies you're using it while traveling — check the fine print if your travels involve the USA.
- Travel insurance is not health insurance, and travel insurance is not typically intended to be your primary medical coverage. Depending on the nature of your medical issues, travel insurers may opt to patch you up, then fly you back to your home country for that country's public system to handle your other issues.
- You may already have travel insurance through your credit card or bank — before purchasing a new plan, review any offerings from your credit card(s) and bank to see if you're already covered.
- So-called 'annual' plans typically cover frequent, short trips, not one long trip as most nomads tend to take. Coverage is typically 30-45 days, but may be up to 60 days. Look at the length of each trip, not the total length of coverage.
- Be aware that some insurance companies offer a 'free look' period (which is another term for the 'cooling-off period' a company is required by law to offer in some countries). This may be anywhere from 7 to 30 days, and in most cases they'll offer a refund if you're not satisfied.

Having said all that, here are a number of companies offering travel insurance that are worth researching (in alphabetical order):

- **Allianz** — offers the TravelSmart app to manage your policy, file claims, and get specific information. Their Classic Plan includes free coverage for children 17 and under when traveling with a parent or grandparent. Annual plans available. Available to US residents only. Learn more at allianztravelinsurance.com.
- **Atlas Travel Insurance** — Offered by Tokio Marine HCC, they offer coverage to people worldwide for up to a year, and the plan is renewable for non-US citizens if your travels don't include the US. A Multi-Trip option is available as well. Learn more at hccmis.com/atlas-travel-insurance.
- **AXA Assistance USA** — Offers an adventure insurance plan that reimburses you for lost diving days and golf rounds, among other things. Available to US residents only, and only for trips of up to 60 days. Learn more at axatravelinsurance.com.
- **British United Provident Association (BUPA)** — offers the myCard app to display your insurance card, policy information, and connect you to a 24-hour emergency service. Covers many holiday activities and sports on the standard plan. Covers travel worldwide, and available to people around the world. Learn more at bupaglobal.com/en/travel-insurance.
- **Cigna Global Health Insurance** — offers 'expat health insurance', and available to people around the world. Check out their Cigna Envoy Mobile App to view and print ID cards, review and check claims, and so on. Learn more at cignaglobalhealth.com.
- **Clements** — available to "expatriates residing outside their country of citizenship for at least 6 months per year", with options to exclude the US and Canada to save on premiums. Learn more at clements.com/intl-health/individuals/globalcare.

- **Generali Global Assistance (formerly CSA Travel Protection)** — very quick quote process. Only available to residents of the US, and not available in all states. Learn more at generalitravelinsurance.com.
- **Geo Blue Travel Insurance** — get insurance excluding or including the US as part of their XPLORER plan. The site offers plans as an "independent licensee of the Blue Cross and Blue Shield Association". Be aware insurance start dates are only about twice a month instead of the usual 'whenever you choose'. Learn more at geobluetravelinsurance.com.
- **Global Rescue** — focusing on evacuation and rescue services, but also offering several general insurance plans. Learn more at globalrescue.com.
- **IM Global** — among their many plans, check out their Global Medical Insurance, which offers long-term (one year or longer) comprehensive medical insurance for 'global citizens'. Available to people worldwide. Learn more at imglobal.com/expat-insurance or imgeurope.co.uk.
- **Integra Global** — claims to "create tailored insurance plans for expats". Use their yourHealth app to access your ID card, submit a claim, create an emergency health record, etc. Available to people worldwide. Learn more at integraglobal.com.
- **Protect Your Bubble** — this is gadget, jewelry, and laptop insurance made simple. Available for UK residents only. Learn more at uk.protectyourbubble.com.
- **Safety Wing** — "The World's First Insurance For Digital Nomads, By Digital Nomads". Automatically extends like a subscription, with one price point for people ages 18-39 (other ages available). Health and travel benefits. Learn more at safetywing.com.
- **Seven Corners** — check their Liaison Continent plan for up to six months of coverage or Liaison Majestic plan for long-term options (up to a year, renewable for two more years). Several deductibles available. Available to most people worldwide, some states and countries excluded. Learn more at sevencorners.com.

- **Travelex** — check their Travel Select plan for trips of up to 364 days, which also covers kids under 18. They also offer expedited passport services for Americans as well as International Driving Permits. Available to people worldwide. Learn more at travelexinsurance.com.
- **Truetraveller** — an option for European residents only, and can be purchased after you've left. Activity packs can cover 'Adventure' activities (like dog sledding or bicycle polo) and 'Extreme' activities (like American football or barefoot water skiing). You'll want to go through their other options to ensure you get the coverage you want (coverage for baggage and personal effects is not standard). Learn more at truetraveller.com.
- **World Escapade** — Available to people worldwide except for US residents. Non-medical and medical travel insurance available. Learn more at worldescapade.com/en.
- **WorldNomads** — arguably one of the best-known options thanks to their affiliate program. Beyond the usual insurance offerings, over 150 popular activities can be covered through their various options (exact activities will vary based on your country of residence). Available to people worldwide, and can be purchased after you've left. Learn more at worldnomads.com.

Do I really need to buy insurance, though? I've met many nomads that never bothered with travel insurance for one reason or another. Either they were lucky to be completely healthy, they chose to stay in countries where medical costs were lower and could be paid out of pocket, or they had bad experiences with insurance companies in the past.

To be sure, plenty of nomads go without travel insurance, but that doesn't mean you should. Being airlifted back to your home country can cost $50,000 or more, and your chances of being fully compensated by the responsible parties in an accident is slim to none in many countries. At the very least, get some quotes.

It's about here that I need to tell you about one person I'd trust to help me navigate this complex world. His name is Andrew Jernigan, and he runs the site international-care.com. Schedule a free consult through the website to take advantage of years of experience of both being a nomad and selling insurance. As of publication, he was working on an insurance plan specifically for digital nomad at insurednomads.com, and depending on when you read this, it may (or may not) be fully developed and ready for sale. It's worth a look.

Medical tourism

What's this I've heard about 'medical tourism'? Medical tourism is essentially travel with the primary purpose of getting medical work done. Seeing the local sights will have to defer to appointments and follow-up visits. Hospitals and clinics may offer surgeries and procedures for a fraction of what they might cost in more developed countries. You need to do your research here and check the quality of the hospital or clinic you visit. Many, such as some large Thai hospitals in Bangkok, are even accredited by American organizations. You can typically find doctors who speak English well and were trained overseas, which is definitely a good thing to check in a country like Thailand where local qualification standards are subpar.

One warning: Don't book packages through websites dedicated to medical tourism unless you really need your hand held throughout the entire process. They will charge you double or more what the procedure actually costs for having someone meet you at the airport, book a hotel for you, and so on. Just Google hospitals or clinics at your destination, or see if you can identify which hospital they'll be taking you to. If you're less confident, Google English-speaking hospitals or clinics in the country you're visiting. Plenty of people have gone before you, and you can come up with a list of reputable places. Embassy websites are also good for this. Most medical facilities worldwide will have some English, so you can usually call or e-mail the clinic or hospital you want to visit and set up appointments yourself. This is a good way to get any number of elective procedures done at a low cost.

Book your travel

We're getting close to the light at the end of the tunnel! By now, you should know when you'll be able to leave and where you want to go, so it's time to book your travel and find a place to live.

If you're just testing out the lifestyle, you may decide the next state, province, or city over is as far as you need to go. That's perfectly fine (and may mean you can drive or take a bus / train there!).

If you're leaving the country, it's probably time to book a plane ticket. While there are plenty of third-party aggregators out there (google.com/flights, expedia.com, skyscanner.com, and kayak.com being four worthy ones), these days there may not be that much of a difference in price between them and directly booking on the airline itself. Also, if a problem arises, that third-party aggregator and the airline will too often point the finger at the other party, making it more difficult to figure out who's to blame.

Remember to look at and consider your luggage while booking the ticket. Jennifer Booker Smith notes, "Some low cost airlines will consider your personal item to be your one carry on. Some weigh your carry on. Some are very strict with checked bags, but only limit carry on dimensions. Others weigh your carry-on pretty much every time. They each have their own quirks."

If this all sounds like the silliest thing you can imagine, I'd agree. According to an estimate by IdeaWorksCompany, airlines made a projected $109 billion off of 'ancillary fees' in 2019. This is the category of fees on things like oversized luggage, unaccompanied minor services, printing a boarding pass, food on the plane, sale of frequent flyer miles, seat assignment fees, and so on. Having very specific policies in fine print offers plenty of chances for a 'gotcha' moment, and low-cost carriers such as EasyJet, RyanAir, WizzAir, and Spirit Airlines are notorious for these.

One additional hassle: some countries or airlines require showing 'proof of onward travel'. This is often interpreted as having a round-trip ticket, but can also be a ticket to leave the country . (A train ticket or bus ticket may work, but these can be difficult or impossible to get before you arrive.) The strictest countries for this are Brazil, Indonesia, New Zealand, Peru, the Philippines, the United Kingdom, and the United States, while other travelers have reported issues with Mexico, Panama, and Thailand.

It's not just the *countries* that are responsible, though. The airlines may require proof as well, because the airline is often responsible for returning anyone that's refused entry back to where they started.

Three common strategies to avoid 'onward travel' issues at the airport, from most to least effort:
- Plan out your entire trip in advance, buying your round-trip or one-way tickets months ahead of time.
- Buy a round-trip, super-cheap ticket that leaves the country, or any ticket with your airline miles / points — then cancel it and get a refund. Avoid doing this with any low-cost European carrier like WizzAir, who are under no obligation to offer refunds within 24 hours.
- Use a service like bestonwardticket.com, which buys a plane ticket (on their credit card), then sends you the ticket with confirmation code. Use that as proof of onward travel. You never actually fly anywhere with the ticket they buy — 24-48 hours after purchase, they cancel the ticket and get their money back.
    - (You may have heard of Fly Onward, a service that used to do the same thing. They closed in early 2018.)

As you're booking, check how many stops or transfers it'll take to get you from point A to point B — and how long you'll be sitting at an airport between flights. Fewer and shorter stops are obviously better, and it might be worth paying a bit extra to avoid a long layover or an awkward arrival time! Consider the time of day, both when you're leaving and arriving. Nancie McKinnon offers a great tip: "I always try to arrive at my destination in the morning or early afternoon. Less stress navigating an unknown city or town during daylight hours." Arriving after dark can make it a lot more difficult to buy a SIM card, find food, convert currency, get onto the right bus / train, or find a legitimate taxi. Remember that arrival and departure times are always based on the local time zones, not where you are now.

While there are some 'travel hacking' websites offering 'error fares' or 'secret fares', these are never guaranteed to get you from where you're starting to where you're going. If you're really flexible with when you leave and love searching for these sorts of fares, head to flyertalk.com, flynous.com, or secretflying.com.

As frequent flyers go, you'll quickly discover which of the three alliances you're most likely to fly: oneworld.com, staralliance.com, or skyteam.com/en. If you decide to put in the effort to collect and manage frequent flyer miles, ensure you're only flying on the airlines in that alliance. For the few times a year we actually fly, it's not worth it to restrict our searches to 1/3 (or less) of the world's airlines, and it's *definitely* not worth paying more for a flight just to collect some points or miles that *may* become useful someday. If you fly a lot and are willing to invest some time and effort to learning the system, you might find it useful.

Wrapping it all up

By this point…

- You know where you're headed and you've booked your ticket(s).
- Your passport is current, and you're aware of any visa requirements.
- You've sorted out medications, vaccinations, and given notice if you're leaving your job.
- You've begun to think about, and do, the kind of work you might do once you arrive at your destination.
- You have decided whether to find a place to stay before you arrive, or wait until you get there and play it by ear.
- The question of travel insurance has been settled.
- Your essential paperwork is in a safe place with several copies that can be easily accessed.

Are you getting excited? You should be! There's not a lot left to do at this point to prepare — but we're not finished yet.

.

Step 5: Gear up and slim down

Give yourself a pat on the back if you've made it this far. Planning and researching for an entirely new way of life is no easy task, and it can look really scary to leave everything you know.

Where previous steps were all about the 'software' (the planning, research, etc.), this step is all about the 'hardware' (getting you and your stuff from A to B). The two big questions in this step are **What** do I pack? and What do I pack it **in**? Your answer to one of these questions will guide your answer to the other.

Before we answer either question, let's consider some standard options and define some terms:
- **Laptop bag** — often considered a personal item by airlines, these padded bags are good for holding your computer and its accessories. Bear in mind that personal items are usually expected to go below the seat in front of you.
- **Backpack** — most likely a carry-on, but possibly a personal item depending on its size. Since backpacks come in all shapes and sizes, they're measured in liters to indicate their capacity.
- **Personal item** — a smaller thing that can be taken on-board, and must fit under the seat in front of you. Bags like a laptop computer, purse, small backpack, briefcase, camera case, or other small items are generally acceptable, though some airlines have specific size requirements. Any items carried on-board will be subject to X-rays and inspection before boarding the plane.
- **Carry-on luggage** — a smaller piece of luggage you're allowed to take on a plane, and is usually stored in the overhead compartments. Any items carried on-board will be subject to X-rays and inspection before boarding the plane.

- **Checked luggage** — a larger piece of luggage that's checked into the plane's baggage hold. They're also X-rayed for dangerous materials, but more stuff is allowed in checked luggage since you can't access it during the flight.

For your first trip, start by figuring out what luggage you already have that's in good working condition. There's no reason to buy something new (or even new to you) if you have something you can use. Is a wheel missing or a zipper broken? Fix it or throw it away — luggage takes enough of a pounding as it is.

Next, let's answer one of those two questions — *what to pack* and *what to pack it in?* Again, your answer to one will guide your answer to the other. Whether you end up choosing a big backpack or two suitcases per person, **make it a personal goal to push, pull, or carry everything you own from A to B in one load**. If you have kids, that includes everything they need as well. Why? Mobility, for one, but if you take so much stuff with you that you can't carry it all in one load, there's a very good chance you'll be paying extra each and every time you fly.

Another reason is ease of travel — being able to carry everything you travel with makes it easier to pack up and go. If you want to feel particularly mobile, aim for just the carry-on and the personal item. If you already have some luggage (even if it's missing a wheel), use it to get a sense of just how much stuff actually fits in it.

Let's dive a little deeper into luggage, and what to look for if you're buying.

Personal item

- A 'personal item' is what airlines call a shoulder bag, purse, laptop bag, or other 'small item'. The maximum size on most (but not all) airlines is 22 cm x 25 cm x 43 cm (9 inches x 10 inches x 17 inches). It's pretty rare to have the dimensions of a bag hold things up as you're checking in on a flight, but it can happen. As weight goes, it's rare to see a specific weight allowance for a personal item, but some airlines will add the weights of the carry-on and personal item together. If they're over the weight limit, one of the bags might have to be checked at an additional cost.
- What's *not* counted as a personal item? Generally, diaper bags, jackets, umbrellas, food and drinks purchased in the airport, canes, strollers, child seats, medical devices, and mobility devices. This could be broken down into the 'stuff humans need to live' category and the 'incidental stuff that takes up almost no space' category. Either way, it's generally exempt from luggage requirements.
- There's no need to *buy* a personal item. You're simply bringing the things you'll want or need while flying on board, or perhaps anything that needs some special protection or handling.

Laptop bag

- Laptop bags are usually padded and durable, and often have hand straps and/or a shoulder strap. It's going to get bounced around, and has to absorb that movement so your computer doesn't. That bag your company gave you or the bag your laptop came with may or may not cut it. If you've never traveled with your laptop bag, give it a try by packing everything that would go and take it for a walk around the block. If it fails that test, get another one.
- Laptop bags usually fall into the 'personal item' category of bags, so they'll need to fit under the seat in front of you on an airplane. On buses or trains, these need to be placed as close to you as possible to avoid any theft issues.

Backpacks

- Many backpacks are designed with specific features for specific purposes. If you're traveling with a laptop, look for a padded sleeve along with ample pockets for all the cords and accessories. Most daypacks (think 10-15 liters) and bigger backpacks (think 50-60 liters) probably won't include a laptop sleeve, but double-check a bag you're about the buy if this is important to you.
- As you're sizing up a backpack, check the fit on the person that'll actually be wearing it. A backpack that perfectly fits a taller man might be painful for a shorter woman to wear. A backpack designed for women typically accounts for a woman's wider hips and a narrower, shorter torso. If you're not physically built like those gendered stereotypes, don't limit yourself to backpacks designed for a single gender.
- Some people like tons of external pockets, while others don't. There's no right or wrong answer as to how many pockets are perfect. Keep in mind that they can be helpful for things like water bottles, snacks, and other things you might want quick access to while you're traveling.
- Good backpacks should be water-resistant or waterproof, regardless of what they're designed to hold. Straps that cross your chest and waist help to balance the load across more of your body, so the bigger the backpack, the more important they become. A carry strap or convertible strap of some kind makes it easier to turn a backpack into a carry-on.
- A high-quality backpack need not cost a ton. Depending on the brand and country, expect to spend anywhere from $50 to $200 for a piece that will last years.

Carry-on / checked luggage

- Luggage can have a soft, fabric shell or a hard polycarbonate shell. Each has their pros and cons — the soft shell can be pushed more easily into place in the overhead bin and is generally lighter, but doesn't provide as much protection to the items inside. The hard polycarbonate shell is the other way around — it gives more protection, but it's bulkier and can't be squeezed into as many places as a soft bag can.
- As wheels go, some people find it easier to push a bag with four wheels that spin freely in all directions. Others will prefer the simplicity of a two-wheeled bag with rollerblade-like wheels. I've had both types and prefer the two-wheeled variety, since the free-spinning wheels are more exposed, and can break or jam more easily.
- Don't buy black luggage. Why? It's so freakin' common. If you must choose a black bag, also buy a bright strap or slap on a bright strip of duct tape to distinguish your bag from others. Anything that instantly makes your bag unique or distinctive is the goal here. You'd be surprised at how many people have a bag just like yours, no matter how distinctive you think it looks.
- Airlines around the world have yet to agree on a universally compliant size for luggage. As of late 2019, the most universally accepted size for a carry-on was 22" by 14" by 9" (58.8cm long by 35.5cm wide by 22.8cm thick), but some international budget airlines may only allow smaller bags.
- For checked bags, the most common measurement tends to be the sum of the height, width, and thickness — so long as your bag's under that magic number (and is the correct weight!), you'll be fine. While it's not a universally accepted size, 158 centimeters and 23 kilograms (62 inches and 50 pounds) is a good place to start. Remember to measure *including* the wheels, straps, handles, etc. — after all, that's how the airlines will be measuring.

- When you're shopping for luggage, bring a measuring tape and measure things for yourself. Even the best luggage in the world has some fluctuations in size during manufacturing, or the tags might mention the *internal* size. The last thing you want is for the check-in agent to pull out their measuring tape and reveal you're a half-inch too large to fly without paying an extra fee (yes, this really can happen).
- Go beyond what's available at your local department store / mall and look online as well — but keep it simple. There's no need for your luggage to have fancy add-ons like external batteries, GPS trackers, and so on.
- A solid piece of luggage can cost anywhere from $50 to $200 and can last you for years.

Can I go carry-on only? Yes, but this will naturally limit how much you can bring with you. If you're looking to avoid checking any bags, it'll be easier if you're going to warmer climates and are fine with only a handful of outfits. Long-term nomads may find it difficult to work with this limited amount of space, but if you're keen, try it anyway!

How should I organize my bags? One common suggestion is to use packing cubes — essentially fabric bags that zip closed. Some nomads will put similar items into such cubes, while others might pack a single complete outfit into a cube (making it easy to grab one outfit at a time). You might use packing cubes to separate clean stuff from dirty stuff (I personally keep a supply of plastic bags to handle the dirty or wet stuff). It's just a matter of which style you like the best, and there's no one right answer for everyone. Once you're on location, your luggage turns into a chest or dresser of sorts, so the organization there matters more to many.

What to pack

As you might have guessed, there is no one universal packing list out there. Each person's trip is unique and goes to different destinations, with different people, different sized bags and for different lengths of time. As you're looking at what you might pack, remember that many things can be obtained where you're going as well. The calculation in my brain looks like this:

- If it's more expensive, more critical to daily life, and harder to replace (like a spare computer charger), it's much more likely to be packed.
- If it's less expensive, less critical to daily life, bulkier, or heavier (like a frying pan), it's much less likely to be packed and more likely to be re-bought at the new location.

What exactly is 'expensive' or 'harder to replace'? While that's up to you to determine for yourself and your own sense of value, a personal starting place is about $10 per kilogram *or* something that would take more than an hour to find or shop for. The bar will be higher if I'm flying (where weight is carefully measured and it costs a lot if a bag is overweight), and lower if I'm taking a bus or train (where weight isn't measured and it's just a matter of getting everything in the bag).

Here's a rough packing guide to get you going. As you'll quickly realize, it's far from a universal list, but it will give you at least a starting point to work from.

Absolute essentials
- Passport and other ID's
- Debit / credit cards
- A4 / Letter-size folder of important paperwork

Tech
- Unlocked smartphone
- Laptop computer, charger(s), cords
- Camera, memory cards, batteries, chargers, cords
- Kindle, tablet or e-reader (for games, reading e-books, etc.)
- External battery / power pack
- External mouse
- Headset (for voice calls)
- A USB stick / USB drive (for transferring files between computers)
- A power strip / surge protector
- Plug adapter (to change flat plugs to round plugs, or vice versa)

Clothes
- Underwear (a single-digit number)
- T-shirts (a single-digit number)
- 1 or 2 sweatshirts / hoodies / sweaters / pullovers
- 1 jacket (light or heavy, depending on where you're going)
- 2-3 pairs of jeans / trousers
- Socks (a single-digit number of pairs)
- 1-3 pairs of shoes / sandals (wear your heaviest pair onto the plane)
- 1 formal / dressy outfit (optional)

Toby Richardson suggests: "Bring a white, long sleeve button up if you're toying with the idea of teaching English anywhere."

Health, medicine, and toiletries
Bear in mind that you can pick up a lot of stuff locally (unless you simply must have a certain brand from your home country — don't assume every brand can be found everywhere).

- Small bottle of aspirin or ibuprofen, in the original bottle (unlabeled pills in a plastic bag can look suspicious)
- Vitamins, minerals, or other supplements
- Bandages, antibiotic ointment, nail clippers, small pair of scissors
- Backup pair of glasses in a hard plastic case (if you wear them)
- Contact lenses, solution, copy of the prescription (if you wear them)
- Birth control / sex stuff (condoms, personal lubricant, birth control pills)
- Beard trimmer / hair trimmer
- Comb and/or hair brush
- Makeup, facial cleansers, or other specialized toiletries and healthcare products
- Eye mask and ear plugs (keep these in a handy outer pocket in your carry-on if you'll be using them during the flight / train / bus)
- Microfiber, yoga, or travel towel (**not** a fluffy, cotton one, since those take up a lot of space)

Depending on your flexibility, you might find one product can serve several uses. Toby Richardson mentions, "If you're a guy with short hair, you can easily substitute soap, shampoo, conditioner, moisturizer, shaving cream and hair product, for the combination of liquid soap and moisturizer. The soap will clean everywhere and can clean your hair too. A tiny bit of moisturizer in your hair afterwards will act as product and substitute for the lack of conditioner."

Other important stuff
- Ziploc bags (these have a thousand uses)
- Durable zipper bags or storage cubes (great for organizing smaller stuff in a big bag)
- HDMI cable or Chromecast (lets you connect your computer to big-screen TV)
- Power strip (perfect for powering up everything in one go)

- Plug converters (to go from flat plugs to round plugs, or vice versa)
- Ethernet cable (useful if wifi is unavailable or of questionable security)
- Basic tools (screwdrivers, duct tape, zip ties, needle nose pliers, etc.)
- Office supplies (3x5 cards, pens, permanent markers, dry-erase markers, notebook)

What *not* to pack

Remember that humans around the world eat, drink, shampoo their hair, shave, wear clothes charge their smartphone, wear condoms, have periods, and like to smell good. Very few products needed for everyday life are completely ungettable while traveling.

- Hiking boots — they take up a lot of room and are heavy (if you're actually going to do some serious hiking, wear them when you fly to cut down on luggage weight)
- Dress shoes (same issue)
- More than one formal outfit (unless you're sure you'll actually need them — few will)
- Paper books — it's one thing to take a couple of them, but more than a few can begin to take up a fair bit of room and weight
- Pots, pans, or lots of other kitchen stuff (they're heavy and bulky, and they'll either be in the apartment where you're going or can be purchased once you arrive.)
- Knives, weapons, pepper spray, or other self-defense items (they might be illegal where you're going — once you've arrived, you can look for something small and sprayable. WD-40 or some other noxious chemical can be a great deterrent!)

What you might want to pack
- Toby Richardson points out: "As a tall guy (6'7"/2m) I always make sure to bring pants and a long sleeve shirt from home as the only option in Asia or South America for my height is to get tailored clothes." Tailored clothes aren't *bad*, mind you, but they'll inevitably be more expensive than simply going to the store.

Wrapping it all up
What to pack and how to pack it is an art form. With time, you'll almost be able to do it in your sleep. You'll also quickly learn what you're not using and what not to pack in future. Avoid paying overweight fees and you'll be a much happier camper.

Step 6: The Big Move and settling in

This is probably the most nerve-wracking part of this journey, even if you're just testing the lifestyle out. Deep breath here — you can do this.

The final countdown

There are a few more things to do before leaving, so consider this the final checklist:

7 days before leaving

Make your last weekly / big trip to the grocery store. Your goal here is to get everything you want without leaving food behind or wasting anything.

Register with your embassy. While embassies are often limited in what they can do for their citizens, it's still a good idea to register and let them know you'll be traveling.
- Americans, head to step.state.gov.
- Australians, head to smartraveller.gov.au.
- Brits, the Foreign & Commonwealth Office's (FCO) LOCATE online consular registration system was closed down on 14 May 2013. Head to gov.uk/guidance/how-to-deal-with-a-crisis-overseas for info on what to do if you have any problems while abroad.
- Canadians, head to travel.gc.ca/travelling/registration.
- Kiwis, head to safetravel.govt.nz/register-your-travel.

Share your new address with your friends. Whether they're sending you mail or they might catch up with you one day, let them know where you'll be. If you haven't picked your accommodation yet, be sure to add this to your to-do list once you've done so.

5 days before leaving

Start spending your loose change. Unless you want to keep your coins for collections or playthings, they won't be of much use in another country, and you generally can't convert coins at currency exchange places.

3 days before leaving

If necessary, get the bread, fruits, veggies, or other stuff you'll want for the last few days — anything that has a shorter shelf life. Aim to eat and drink up whatever you have left in the house.

Research the three things you'll need as soon as you arrive: SIM card, cash, and knowing how to get out of the airport and towards wherever you're staying.
- My favorite source for info on SIM cards is over at prepaid-data-sim-card.wikia.com — head there to see which companies offer prepaid SIM cards for your smartphone, and more importantly, which plans are the best value for you. A worthy alternative: worldsim.com, which offers a single SIM card for connecting to networks around the world. It's worth checking out if you'll only be in a given country for less than a week. It's going to be more expensive than local SIM cards, but also more convenient.
- As far as changing money goes, check the rate at your local bank or exchange office — if it's decent, pick some up before you leave, then aim to get more from an ATM after you arrive. At some point, use the Currency app (free on iOS) to show the currency you'll be using in the new country. It'll update online where possible, but otherwise keep the most recent values received while you're offline.
- Getting out of the airport without getting ripped off by a taxi can be harder than you think. If possible, arrange with your Airbnb host to pick you up or figure out which public transportation options connect you to where you're going.

- Alternatively, hire an Uber (or the local taxi app), or determine which line / queue goes to the official, metered taxis.

1 day before leaving

- **Any small change left?** Buy some candy or snacks at the store to stuff in your bag.
- **Download the offline maps** of your destination in Google Maps to your phone. Even if you don't have the internet, the offline maps combined with the GPS signal (which doesn't require the internet) will show your location.
- **If there's a local taxi app** not named Uber or Lyft where you're going, download it to your phone.
- **Open every drawer and door in the place.** The easiest way to forget something is to forget to check everywhere you might have put stuff.
- **The Feast!** Try to make the last couple of meals use up what you have left.

Leaving

- **Do a final cleaning of the place.** This might just be a courtesy or it might be to get your deposit back. Either way, aim to do it well.
- **Meet with your landlord,** Airbnb host, the person caring for your house, or the new tenant — whomever you're leaving the keys with. If you merely need to drop the keys in the mailbox or under the mat, do that instead.
- **Pack it up, pack it in.** Exactly how you're packing will depend on how you're traveling. Traveling by plane means being more conscious of weight, ensuring non-allowed items aren't in your checked bag, and so on.
- **Get to the airport / train station / bus station**. You've probably already weighed the option of public transportation vs. taxi, considering how much stuff you're carrying. If your trip requires multiple transfers or more

than a couple flights of stairs, the extra that you'll pay for a taxi may become worth it.

Checking into your flight

You've probably heard the old line about getting to the airport 2-3 hours before your international flight. This is still true — and the bigger the airport, the earlier you'll want to be there. It's not like there's a penalty for getting there too early (although your flight may not be open for check-in yet). Even with electronic touch-screens facilitating check-in to your flight, there's still the matter of dropping off luggage (and paying a fee if it's overweight). Security can slow things down as well (especially at bigger airports or during weekends or holidays).

The person checking you into your flight will be eyeballing your carry-on bag to ensure it's generally compliant as size goes. It's the *weight* they may end up watching more closely, however. They'll always have the ability to ask you to check it in their allowed-size box, but the less they see it, the better.

While waiting to check-in, I'm usually doing three things with my personal item (be it a laptop bag or backpack) during check-in to make it look smaller and lighter (regardless of its actual size and weight):
- First, while we're still in line, I'll shift anything I can to my back or the side that furthest away from the clerk. This will make it less obvious to them.
- Second, I'll look and act as though the bag weighs almost nothing. That ends up being a combination of a relaxed, neutral face with a casual, comfortable pose.
- Third, once we're at the check-in counter, I'll usually set the bag down by my feet, between the front of my legs and the counter. This makes it almost impossible to see from the raised platform the clerks sit on.

Security is security, and there's no getting around it. There are enough inconsistencies and incongruities that it's difficult to offer tips on this. Most places want your laptop in a separate bin, though tablets are a mixed bag. I also carry my external hard drives in my backpack, which are also usually placed in the tray by themselves. Use as many trays as you need. Aim to get through it as quickly as possible, then get to your gate. Keep your eyes out for the signboards to confirm the gate hasn't changed on you (it does happen), then settle in near a source of electricity if one is handy.

If taking a bus or train, give yourself extra time to buy your ticket, ensure you're at the correct platform, then ensure your luggage is on board and get on. Don't park your luggage out of your sight on a train, and take all the smaller bags on the bus with you.

While you're waiting to board, consider this a perfect time to preview the four stages of culture shock:
- **Honeymoon** — an overwhelmingly positive stage, during which it feels like everything is awesome. You're generally very curious and very open to everything that's new, and you might feel like you can handle anything. This can last anywhere from a few days to a few weeks, but eventually will give way to...
- **Frustration (AKA Negotiation)** — a negative stage based on not understanding the language, what's going on, and so on. The novelty has worn off, and you're looking at what's different between where you are now and where you were. You might feel homesick, confused as to why or how things happen, and even simple things can seem more challenging than they ought to be. This can last a few weeks to a few months, but this will give way to...
- **Adjustment** — a more positive stage where you have become more familiar with the local idiosyncrasies and logic. Things get more comfortable and feel more normal, and you'll soon be able to brush off mistakes or laugh at things that you did before. Your problem-solving skills will have increased, and you can take the local ways into account. After a couple months to several months, this stage will eventually become...

- **Acceptance** — a positive stage where familiarity with your surroundings brings ease. You still won't necessarily understand everything happening around you, but you know you don't have to. You'll appreciate some aspects of the country but be critical of others. You might feel like you belong in this country, and that's a great place to be.

A fifth stage, often called 'Reverse Cultural Shock', is what happens when you return to your former home country and are reminded of your old patterns. Things (and people) that once felt familiar now seem foreign. Worry about that another day (or learn more in Step 8), but know it is a thing that happens.

You are a tourist

One final thing to know before arriving: unless you've planned ahead and acquired another visa (e.g. an Education visa, a Business visa), you are arriving as a *tourist*. Even as a digital nomad, **you are a tourist.** If you're asked 'Business or pleasure?' on a form or by an immigration officer, you say 'pleasure'. Saying *anything* about how you'll be working while in the country can raise red flags to the immigration officer, and might even get you turned away or brought in for more questioning. Answer truthfully: you plan to see the country, enjoy the food, drink some local beers, dance a bit, etc.

OK, so this feels like lying... Digital nomads exist in a legal gray area in many countries. On one level, yes, we are technically working while in the country, and our purpose for coming there is not 100% pleasure. Governments around the world are aware of digital nomads, but *generally*, they do not consider digital nomads a threat. Why? Digital nomads are typically from more affluent countries, we spend a fair bit of money on our housing and food (more than the locals do), and perhaps more importantly, we're not threatening the jobs of locals. (I'd argue the unemployment rate of Chiang Mai has likely gone down somewhat since the Thai city became a hub for digital nomads. The number of coffee shops alone…)

Some countries have or are working to offer 'entrepreneur', 'business', or 'digital nomad' visas, but unless you're arriving on one of them, *you are a tourist*.

Arriving

Welcome to your destination and your new life! The culture shock can begin the moment you arrive, from the new language(s) to the prices you see. Your priorities, in order:
- Get off the plane / train / bus
- Clear immigration, if necessary
- Grab your checked bag(s)
- Clear customs and enter the Arrivals section of the airport (if you flew)
- Get some local currency (exchange some money, use an ATM, or break out the local currency you acquired beforehand)
- Get a local SIM card, then add some credit and a data package to your smartphone
- Find your way to your waiting host, or follow the signs to the bus, train, or taxi out of the airport
- Arrive at your Airbnb / hotel / hostel and get checked in
- Let your friends / family know you made it safely

If you're staying at an Airbnb, most Airbnb hosts are pretty good about giving you a little tour of the apartment, and may also repeat the rules posted on their listing. Use this time to ask questions and otherwise get to know them. Some people host on Airbnb because they like meeting new people, not just for the money you're paying them. Some hosts will actively invite you to events or meals, and they can be a great person to help you out with stuff. Keep on good terms with them.

My wife and I have a ritual related to moving into a new place, mainly because we do it so often. Some common parts:

Day 0
(this is the day you've arrived — if you've arrived late, do what you can today, then get to the rest tomorrow)
- Get keys (one set for each adult where possible), then test the critical locks with all keys, ideally with the host present. If you can't unlock it, watch carefully how the host does it — some locks require a little more push than others.
- Get the wifi password clearly written down somewhere, then log onto it with all devices to confirm it works (and so that the devices remember the password).
- Ask your host about the nearest major grocery store, the nearest bus / metro station, and the nearest mall. Star them in Google Maps.
- If you got SIM cards already, put your traveling partner's phone number(s) in your phone. One person can usually call another, then wait until their phone starts ringing. No need to answer, though — hang up, then look in your recent calls and save their number.
- Take pictures of the place before you settle in (preferably showing your suitcases to confirm the date with the picture's metadata). Beyond showing the conditions of the apartment on that date, it's helpful if you opt to rearrange things and need to put things back in order before leaving. Note any minor issues with some close-up pictures, and address any major issues with your host as soon as possible.
- Open the windows and let in some fresh air.
- Do an inventory of what's there — is anything important missing or not up to a reasonable, usable quality? Check for pots, pans, what sort of appliances are present, etc. Ask the host for what's missing or add it to your shopping list.
- Test the doors, windows, locks, appliances, electronics, A/C or heat sources, etc. Let the host know immediately if anything important doesn't work as expected.

- Get rid of squeaks (use WD-40 or oil) or non-level tables that rock back and forth (use shims or pieces of cardboard). This might be a personal preference, but these are two things that drive me crazy.
- Do a shopping trip for the basics — just enough for a day or so unless you're feeling ambitious.
- Clean anything that isn't sparkling.
- Setup your workspace.

Day 1 (your first full day at the new place)
- Figure out your coffee or tea ritual, if you drink coffee or tea.
- Unpack your stuff — some people prefer living out of drawers or shelves rather than suitcases. As you're settling in, find the balance between keeping to your old habits and not losing yourself in the new country's offerings.
- Write down your address and host's phone number on a card in case of emergency, then put one in each wallet, purse, manbag, etc. Be sure every person has one with them whenever they leave the house.
- Get copies of key(s), if needed.
- Rearrange furniture as necessary — the goal here is to make the place work for you.
- Start enjoying the new city a bit! Book a walking tour, pick up a public transport card (or some tickets, as appropriate), look at the maps or brochures available to you, or make it a point to visit the local tourist information office.
- Join some local Facebook groups, Meetups, the local Couchsurfing groups, and so on. Jan Robinson mentions, "Some people use Tinder purely for friendship and sightseeing purposes."
- Update your location on Facebook. Some groups only let in members that are locals to prevent spam.
- Do a more thorough grocery / shopping trip.
- Figure out how the trash and recycling works. As you're walking around, look for how the trash and recycling are separated. If it's not clear, ask your host.

Day 2 (2nd full day in the new city)
- Hit up some touristy hotspots — go on, be a tourist! Allow yourself some time today to just be in the town.
- Go through the lists from day 0 and day 1 — did you get to everything?
- Figure out your best mix of work, sleep, and free time. This will not, and should not, look like it did in your old life. If you've been meaning to try sleeping in and working late, start getting into the habit now!

Day 3 (3rd full day in the new city)
- Discover the local stores, get comfortable shopping the local way, and begin figuring out what might be more difficult to come by here and how to adjust to it. Ask your host where they find the specific thing(s) you're looking for.
- Begin exploring the city — how far you go is up to you, but the goal is to see what Google Maps isn't showing you. Good restaurants? Hardware stores? A one-dollar or one-euro store?
- If you haven't yet, make it a point to connect with local nomads / expats today. Is there a Meetup from meetup.com or a Facebook group getting together? Now's a great time to connect with people offline.
- Begin getting into a routine, if you haven't already.
- Figure out whether the city runs early or late — by this I mean whether places close early or late, whether places are closed on Sundays or open as usual, whether bars are open late or close at 9pm, and so on.

Wrapping things up

There are a thousand and one other details that, and although they're about travel and international travel in general, they aren't really about being a digital nomad. Observing the human condition, whether haggling is a thing, how people communicate, how the place smells, what buildings look like, how much personal space you get from other people, jetlag (it'll disappear within a couple of days), how people fold or count their money... These are all part of that 'honeymoon' phase where everything is new.

I won't spoil the rest of them for you — there's always a transition period, it's always a relatively stressful time, and there's no easy way around it. Your best bet is to manage it as best you can, plan what you can in advance, understand the stress will pass, and try to take it easy for the first few days while you adapt.

Step 7: Start enjoying your new life

You're now a few days to a week into your new life — and yes, you are a digital nomad now. There's been a lot of change over the last couple of weeks, but things are slowly beginning to settle down. There's still a lot more to see and do and try, and you can't wait to get to it all!

This step will be the shortest section — a lot of the hard work is done, but naturally, there's plenty more to do that'll be unique to your circumstances. Making your ideal life will take time, effort, and commitment. If you've made it this far, you've put in a lot of time and effort to that end, so pat yourself on the back.

Celebrate the hard work you've done thus far, then get started on creating a routine that fits you. It's yours to choose, but you'll still *need* a routine. We'll get to that in a minute — for now, let's get to the next worksheet.

Worksheet #11: Now that you're settled in...

Date: _____

Find this at becomingadigitalnomad.com/worksheet11. Print a copy and complete offline, or complete online, then print or save.

How many days ago did you move in? _____

How's it going so far?

_____

What's been the biggest moment of culture shock?

_____

How's work going? What are you working on?

_____

What new gigs can you take to make some more money?

_____

What skills do you need to brush up on, or hire someone to teach you?

_____

How are the locals?

_____

How are things back 'home'? Do you miss anything?

_____

Look ahead 6 months — where do you want to be?

_____

As stuff goes...

It's practically a law of traveling. There's bound to be something you want or need that will be difficult to find. Maybe it's a special brand of candy you love, or a specific office supply, or the like. Even with extensive research, there's no way to know what these things will be (or what you'll miss) ahead of time. Accept it, consider it a treasure hunt to find it, search for the best alternative available locally, or make a version of it yourself.

Remember to question the conventional ways you're expected to use things — as a nomad, you'll find yourself hanging a curtain with little more than some clothesline and push pins. I've made an emergency arm sling out of plastic grocery bag, used a compass (the type used for making circles) to fix a shower head, and once used a broom, a Coke bottle and some duct tape to open a locked door that locked from inside.

As home maintenance goes, it's not your responsibility to *fix* the inevitable issues that come with housing anywhere you go. It *is* your responsibility to let the owner know, and more importantly, adapt the house to be comfortable to your needs and wants within reason. Look at the place itself to see how much the owner is likely to care — if there's already lots of holes in the walls, they're unlikely to notice or care about a few more. If the wall is immaculate, it'll be pretty obvious.

You've already read my suggestions to do an inventory of what a place has, then going out to stock up. Over time, this can feel like you're stocking someone's place for them. I get that. We've bought — and left behind — plenty of things like frying pans (the one in the house was a nightmare to clean since everything stuck to it), small heaters (cold winters), fans (because the only air-conditioner in the apartment was in the living room, not the bedroom), silverware (no butter knives? Seriously?), and so on. Over the course of 2-3 months that we're at a place, the amount we paid for these things comes to pennies per day, but they made our lives easier, more enjoyable, more comfortable, etc. You won't need or be able to take these things with you, so make them part of the Purge before you leave, or just leave them behind for the next people to enjoy.

Wait, what's the Purge? The Purge is my name for what to do in the days before leaving one place — it's a time to look at everything you own and see what needs to be left behind, what needs to be donated, and what needs to stay with you. This isn't limited to anything you've bought while at this place — are any clothes getting too worn out? Have you realized you haven't used something in a long time? Did something stowaway from a previous trip?

Several things are generally easy to find, have a multitude of functions / purposes, and are great to have on hand for any number of reasons:
- Duct tape — from making things stay in place to attach stuff to other stuff, I always have a roll in one of my bags. Use it to strengthen a window in a hurricane (apply a spider web pattern), get geeky and make a wallet or customized case from it if you want, or just cover a wart with it.
- WD-40 (or another sort of spray lubricant) — if it needs to move and isn't, or if it squeaks and it shouldn't, this is useful. Also good for removing sticker residue (usually needs to soak in, though). May prevent and block metallic things from rusting.
- White vinegar — great for cleaning almost anything. Dilute it in some cases, or go full-strength for full power. Also stops itching from mosquito bites, loosens screws, removes gum, wax, and sticker residue, unclogs shower heads, and more.
- Baking soda — combined with equal parts vinegar, it unclogs drains. In a paste with water, it's a toothpaste, exfoliant, and sunburn relief. By itself, it's indigestion relief, cleans carpets, deodorizes refrigerators, cleans mildew in

bathrooms, and can put out small grease fires. Mixed with equal parts salt, it keeps ants out.
- Coconut oil — beyond being a healthier cooking oil, it's also a fine massage oil, personal lubricant, a natural moisturizer, diaper rash guard, and constipation relief. The whiter, the better.
- Plastic shopping bags — beyond their obvious function of holding stuff, they're good for separating dirty / wet clothes from clean ones. If necessary, they can also make an emergency bowl, a rope (tape, tie, or braid together), and so on.

Speaking of stuff — what about shopping?

Shopping offline remains your best bet for finding plenty of options without worrying about shipping, customs, and so on. The upside is immediate access. The downsides are limited selection, potentially higher prices, and a tougher time finding exactly what you're looking for. I personally look at shopping offline as a reason to explore a city's malls, the back streets, and so on... but this is a personal choice, and not everyone will have the time or interest.

Shopping online may be more hassle than it's worth, especially in countries with less reliable postal delivery services. International shipping is expensive, and surprise customs fees can prevent a shipment from reaching you or force you to find the post office in person. If there's a local site locals trust, by all means give it a try. It's just not our first place to look for something.

Although plenty of places offer international shipping, one place for many to start will be amazon.com/global, if the country you're in doesn't have its own dedicated store (over 15 different countries do). Through this website, shipping to 100+ countries is possible and offers a pretty wide variety of stuff.

For more esoteric stuff, aliexpress.com (run by the Chinese company Alibaba) is another great option. The quality of these Chinese-made products can vary dramatically, so read the reviews and descriptions to ensure you get what you expect.

As addresses go, aim to give your address in the local language as it appears on the postal mail, not how it appears on the Airbnb listing or on Google Maps. Every country's system has its own idiosyncrasies, but packages that use local addresses in the local language have a better chance of being delivered. If you're unsure how to type the address in the local language, look at the mail at your place or use a site like typeit.org to click or type the non-English characters you need.

Avoiding censorship

More than a few countries censor the internet (or programs that rely on the internet) for religious, ideological, or other reasons. Consider getting a VPN (Virtual Private Network) to encrypt your internet traffic by routing it through a different server, bypass any local internet censorship, and keep your internet browsing private from your internet provider, host, or government. These usually have a monthly fee, and have discounts available if you pay for a year at a time. We currently use nordvpn.com and have used privateinternetaccess.com in the past.

Creating routine

As I said earlier, routine is important — making the most of your time is even more important now that it's all yours to deal with. At a minimum, your routine should take into account the following:

- The time you do your best work
- Any time(s) you need to be at meetings or online for a specific purpose
- Your partner's and/or children's needs
- When you *naturally* choose to get up / go to bed
- When you want to socialize
- The reality of office and store hours
- Meditation and/or workout time
- Meal times (doubly important with family)

Some folks may find they prefer some aspects of the 9-to-5 schedule — at least, the part where they work during the morning and afternoon and leave the evenings free for whatever. Others might make it more of a 1-to-9 sort of schedule — sleep in, eat some lunch, then get to work. It's entirely up to you (and whomever else you're traveling with) — the sky's the limit.

Part of that routine means figuring out the best times to do the menial, boring stuff — when the trash cans have to be put out, where the recycling goes, when the grocery store is less busy (or just what times work best for you).

Spring cleaning

Speaking of routine, once every 6 months as a nomad, do a spring cleaning. Take *everything* out of all your bags. Clean the inside of your bags. Try on all the clothes you own to ensure they still fit. Check for holes, then repair or dispose of those clothes. Match up all the power or connecting cords to tech you still own, and check that all the tech still works as intended. Even as a nomad, stuff can still accumulate.

Keeping track of finances

Finances and budgets can be tricky things for digital nomads. On one hand, some things are much cheaper than you're used to — once you've gotten rid of your car, you won't need car insurance or gas/petrol. Even with a frequently used bus or metro ticket, the 'transportation' line item in the budget is likely to go way down. Some line items may go up, and some expenses may fall into one of those tricky 'other' categories. Use the upcoming worksheet to help.

Worksheet #12: Stay on budget!

Date: _____

Find this at becomingadigitalnomad.com/worksheet12. Print a copy and complete offline, or complete online, then print or save.

Compare your actual spending with your projected amounts from worksheet #6.

For month starting _____

and ending _____ :

Expenses	Amount spent	Amount projected
Housing		
Utilities (electricity, water, gas)		
Credit card payments		
School loans		
Entertainment		
Groceries		
Eating out		
Alcohol / parties		

Household needs (cleaning supplies)		
Clothes		
Health / wellness (vitamins, gym membership, medications)		
Travel / Health Insurance		
Transportation (car payment, car insurance, gas / petrol, public transportation)		
Internet / phone		
Costs of doing business:	———	———
Your website(s) (web hosting, domain names, web developer)		
Virtual assistant or other service providers		
Software products / online or subscription services		
Other costs of doing business		
Other expense #1 (_____)		
Other expense #2 (_____)		
Other expense #3 (_____)		

Other expense #4 (_____)		
Other expense #5 (_____)		
TOTAL		

How did you do? Let the actual numbers calibrate your estimates from one month to the next, and don't beat yourself up too badly if your projections were way off. Be aware that certain line items will change dramatically from one place to the next, but others won't. In other cases, you might choose to spend the same amount wherever you go, but accept it won't go as far as it did somewhere else.

Taking care of yourself, and taking it in stride

The term of the day is 'self-care': taking care of your physical, emotional, mental, and spiritual self. The digital nomad lifestyle can take a toll on all four of those aspects at a time when you're separated from all of your usual support structures, so take the extra time to give yourself the care you need.

What to watch out for (and a possible reason)?
- Feeling anxious about the future / unknown (incomplete planning)
- Depressed (not sleeping well, not feeling successful)
- Loneliness (disconnected from friends and family)
- Being isolated (not networking or making local friends)
- Feeling tired of change (traveling too fast or changing things too fast)

What does self-care look like?
- Sleeping 6-8 hours a day in a comfortable bed with a good pillow
- Staying physically active by walking, jogging, working out, etc.
- Staying connected to friends and family (both online and offline)
- Drinking plenty of clean water (bottled if necessary, purified / filtered if possible)
- Continuing to learn and educate yourself about your interests, your passions, etc.
- Attending religious services (if you're religious)
- Finding an outlet for your stress (yoga, sports, whatever)
- Limiting how much you drink or smoke (and know the signs of addiction)
- Staying aware and street-smart (knowing you're in control of your situation)
- Avoiding excessive junk food / comfort food (eating healthy where possible and embracing the local cuisine)

Along these same lines, there are going to be language barriers, cultural differences, and quirks that catch you off-guard. Maybe you'll get home and realize that wasn't milk you just bought, or maybe you'll get on the wrong line of the subway... going the wrong way... These things happen, and might make for a fun story down the line. For now, just accept that these happen to every digital nomad.

Evaluate how things are going

It's worth taking some time every few months to see how you're doing, whether you're staying on track, meeting your goals, and so on. A few questions to ask yourself (compare your answers to the last time you did this, of course!):

1. On a scale of 1 (saddest) to 10 (happiest), how happy are you?
2. Are you doing what you want, when you want to? If not, why not?
3. Have your bank account balances gone up or down in the past month?

Resources if things are going wrong

It's inevitable that things won't always go to plan, but your inner resilience will usually see you through. Have patience, talk to a friend, head out to a party, take a walk, or enjoy whatever helps you relax.

If the issues go beyond that, it might be time to talk to a professional. This can be problematic as a nomad, where local morals and language barriers can create more problems than they solve. Instead of working with a local psychologist, I'd recommend trying an English-language service that should work anywhere in the world, along with a few professionals that communicate via Skype:

- Talkspace.com — a flat-fee therapy service with over 1,000 licensed therapists. Choose between 'Unlimited Messaging' and 'LiveTalk' Therapy for two different weekly rates. Primarily American therapists who work on American time zones.
- 7cups.com — "free, anonymous and confidential online text chat with trained listeners, online therapists & counselors." A premium plan covers more specific offerings, and apps for Apple and Android are available.
- Betterhelp.com — one flat weekly fee for unlimited sessions with your licensed, accredited professional counselor. Over 2,000 therapists available.
- Breakthrough.com — a more traditional search engine to find mental / emotional health professionals. Lots of information about each therapist. Almost entirely North American-based. Accepts some (but not all) traditional insurance, and you can search by which insurance programs are accepted.
- Dr. Sonia Jaeger has worked as a psychotherapist and clinical psychologist, and she herself is a digital nomad. She speaks English, German, and French. Learn more at sonia-jaeger.com
- Ellen Bard is "a thought leader in productivity, and the challenges of work-life balance in the modern fast-paced, technology-enabled world." Learn more at ellenbard.com.
- Rev. Dr. W. Hunter Roberts has over 25 years of experience and is as smart as they come. Savvy business woman as well as skilled listener. Free first consultation. Learn more at trans-arts.com.

Don't forget where you came from

This will look different for every person, but some things to consider:

- Be proactive in staying connected to your friends and family. Have a set time to connect via phone or Skype, or set something up via e-mail.
- Don't forget to vote! Just because you've left the country doesn't take away that right. Americans, look up votesfromabroad.com to learn the best way to cast absentee or other ballots while abroad.
- Enjoy the holidays from your home country however you like — you may not be physically present to enjoy the proverbial Thanksgiving turkey, but a local restaurants may offer a tempting feast. You can always watch your nephew / niece open presents via Skype, or see how old the family has gotten at Christmas. I've yet to be a place on earth that didn't celebrate New Years Eve in some way. Remember there are plenty of local holidays to enjoy as well — what might pass for a normal day back in your home country might be one of the biggest holidays of the year where you are.
- Read the local newspaper or magazines online, or perhaps blogs kept by locals.
- Make some local foods, drinks, or just whatever's comfortable.

Wrapping it all up

This is your new life. Welcome it. Embrace it. Challenge yourself. Live it. Congratulations — you made it!

Step 8: Coming home

A quick note: when I use 'home' in this chapter, I'm referring to the city you came from, a familiar city, where your family lives, or the like — a familiar place, in other words.

Very few people remain digital nomads for their entire lives, and virtually every digital nomad will return to their home country after a time. This step focuses on seeing your home country through the lens of the digital nomad lifestyle and the experiences you've had, helping you deal with 'reverse culture shock', and reacclimating to a post-digital-nomad life.

The circumstances of returning where you came from can be anywhere from a glorious return involving plenty of pomp and circumstance to a reluctant trip home out of necessity. Perhaps a loved one is getting married, having a child, has passed away, has some sort of medical emergency, or the like. Maybe you enjoyed your time as a digital nomad, but are now ready to settle in, buy a house, or otherwise return to a more traditional lifestyle. Whatever the circumstances, a decision has been made, and life is changing once again.

Look in the mirror — you've changed

Some of the ways you've changed will be obvious enough — gaining or losing weight, getting older, maybe a scar or two. Other ways can't be measured or talked about. You've grown, though. Your attitudes and mindsets are more world-centric. Maybe your political or religious views have changed. Maybe you left single and came back with a spouse and children. It's all part of life, and there's no going back to the way you were.

What is reverse culture shock?

Reverse culture shock is the culture shock of returning to your former homeland, culture, society, or the like. What was familiar and predictable suddenly isn't. It can come from the difficulty in re-adjusting to the culture and values of 'home', but it can also come from memories and nostalgia. Every sense is affected — having experienced the Asian version of *spicy*, the watered-down version at the Asian restaurant close to home just doesn't taste the same.

One common point many digital nomads have made is that it feels like *they've* changed a lot, but the home and people they've *returned* to has barely changed. It's like you were gone for two weeks instead of months or years. People might still be at the same job, going to the same places, or are otherwise are in the same routine they were in.

By this point in your journey, you've probably heard the quote from Mark Twain: "Travel is fatal to prejudice, bigotry, and narrow-mindedness, and many of our people need it sorely on these accounts. Broad, wholesome, charitable views of men and things cannot be acquired by vegetating in one little corner of the earth all one's lifetime." This applies to you… but not necessarily your friends and family. Remarks from friends or family that once seemed fine may now come off as sounding closed-minded, sexist, racist, etc. They haven't had the incredible experiences you've had, so it's highly unlikely they will have dramatically changed while you were away. Accept that you can't change other people, but remember you *can* choose who you spend time with. That crazy uncle can still spout his conspiracy theories, but that doesn't mean you have to listen to them.

Part of this reverse culture shock is observing what you didn't think about before: how loud everything is, how rude (or polite) people are, seeing your privilege on full display, people complaining about inconsequential 'first-world-problems', and so on. It can help to think of 'home' as the next stop on your list, and a place to adjust to as you would to any other place. You never know exactly what life will be like, no matter how much research you do, and this is no different.

Harder or easier?

Plenty of factors can make coming home harder or easier on you:
- Did you choose to return, or was there some force making you return?
- Is home really different from where you've been?
- Is this your first time coming back?
- How long were you away?
- Are people happy you're back, or is your presence making things more difficult?

Home for a few days, for awhile, or forever?

One common question folks back home will ask is 'how long are you here?'. It's a fair question, especially when you've been away for months or years. Is this a permanent return home, or just a temporary visit? Whatever has brought you home may override those questions for awhile, and it's fair to not know at first, but people will want to know eventually.
It's easiest to answer if this is just a short trip to celebrate at a wedding or mourn at a funeral, or if the stay is defined by a season ('I'm just here to enjoy the summer'). The people you care about deserve a straight answer, whatever it may be.

Who wants to hear a story?

Let's just start this off with a mood killer: not everyone wants to hear all your stories, and no one wants to see the 500 selfies you took along the way. Yes, you can (and should) share your experiences as people want to hear them, but avoid making a captive audience listen to your story about that awful diarrhea you had in Thailand.

People that haven't extensively traveled often ask general questions — 'What was your favorite place?', 'Did you have fun?', or 'What was it like?' being three common ones. Treat them as the conversation starters they are, or simply as the polite questions people ask when better ones don't come to mind. Avoid ignoring the questions or giving one-word answers, however.

Do seek out opportunities to talk about your experiences, though — whether this is a chance to address students at your local high school, speak at a local travel group, or be the VIP at a Meetup, the sky's the limit. This might be a chance to promote your blog or your Instagram, but look at it as an opportunity to inspire others in your hometown and enjoy the memories you made.

You won't always think about the life of a digital nomad as being all that exotic. Sometimes that's because there's so much going on you don't take the time to really think about it. Now that you're home, you're probably 'the exotic one' — or you might return home and discover everyone's wrapped up in their own minds and lives and may not be at all curious about what you've been doing. Remember to ask about their lives as well. By comparison it may not sound as interesting (and they'll say as much), but be genuinely curious. Probe a bit. Things that might be mundane to them are likely fascinating to you. You've probably missed out on some aspects of pop culture / games / music / movies / apps, and they might be able to fill you in.

Stay exotic and 'international'

Whatever you enjoyed while traveling, find a way to connect to it while home. International clubs, Toastmasters groups, Meetups, Couchsurfing groups, German beer nights, trips to the Asian food market, foreign movies at the theater — you get the idea. Yes, imports will cost more or be difficult to find — enjoy them as the taste of life you've experience, or use the events / meetups as an excuse to expose your friends to some fellow travel-minded people. If those events or meetups aren't as common as you'd like or you can't find one you want to attend, start your own!

Reconnecting and accepting drift

Friends and family can drift apart. Assuming they know you've come back and are in the same city, it's just as much on them to reconnect as it is on you. If you haven't announced it to the world (or at least via social media and e-mail), now's the time. Share your plans and intentions (as well as you know them), along with the specific things you've been looking forward to doing for awhile now.

You will reconnect with some people and discover your relationship naturally picks up where it was. You'll reach out to others and have a good time, but not feel the strong urge to hang out with them again. Some people will never respond. It happens. Some people are worth the effort to find, of course.

Sometimes, the reality is that you and someone you were close to have drifted too far away from each other. You can always reconnect with somebody, but you might find you don't have a lot to talk about. Acknowledge it, and allow for that to change in the future. You never know when they'll reach out, out of the blue, to mention their vacation plans or ask what you thought of a certain city.

Getting out vs. staying in

Whatever situations or circumstances that brought you back may override these preferences, but do your best to avoid simply staying around the house. It's perfectly acceptable to take some time and sleep or recuperate from a lot of travel, but eventually you'll probably want to see the city. Whether you're more interested in seeing what's changed or what's stayed the same, it'll likely be an interesting journey all the same.

This can be made more challenging if you lack transportation, or if the public transportation in the area leaves something to be desired. Remember to be sensitive to the schedules of the ride-givers, and to pay for gas / fuel / petrol when possible.

Looking back and moving forward

Traveling as a lifestyle has been a great ride, but it's now in the past if you're back for good. It's time to move forward in some way. Ready to start working? Need to find some gigs? Going to start school? Need an apartment? Whatever you're gearing up to do, there's stuff that needs doing. Life has ways of giving you goals to work towards.

But I don't know what I want to do yet! Whatever force brought you home may not have released its grip on you yet. That's fine. If you're only home temporarily, this is irrelevant. If you knew ahead of time that you were going home for awhile, you hopefully geared up for this just like you geared up for the digital nomad journey.

Adulting

Some people will use your coming home as a fresh chance to ask some pointed questions:
- 'So when are you getting married?'
- 'So when are you having kids?'
- 'Did you save any money to put towards buying a house?'
- 'Did you enjoy your vacation?'

The barbs might start flying with questions like:
- 'When are you going to get a real job?'
- 'What's wrong with staying here and settling down?'
- 'Why did you come back if you've got it all figured out?'
- 'Isn't it time you grew up?'
- 'Why do you do *that?*' [where *that* is anything you've started doing as a nomad that you didn't do before]
- 'Isn't traveling dangerous? Did you read that story where…"

Yes, you need to be responsible and able to care for yourself, your spouse, and your child(ren)... but your definition of being an adult never has to match the way your parents / friends / siblings define it! Being an adult does not mean being tied down to a single community, job, or to what you can or can't do.

The diplomatic approach remains the best approach initially, though it's usually the hardest. You might need to walk them through what you do, how you make money from it, and how it's a sustainable job. If what you do is a bit less stable or sustainable, you'll want to emphasize what's been working while acknowledging the issues you've been having. Emphasize the flexibility your job / gigs / routine offers you to truly enjoy life on your terms.

I have yet to meet or hear of a digital nomad whose non-nomadic parents completely understood their lifestyle. You might think your successes speak for themselves, but successes are rarely as public or well-known as you think they are. Also, things we regard as 'successes' in the digital nomad world do not equal 'success' in the traditional world. Your parents might not understand how getting 10,000 followers on your social media is an accomplishment, because they may not see how that puts money in your bank account. Have some talking points at the ready for those questions from earlier.

The worst-case scenario: you're home because you're broke

This does happen to an unfortunate number of digital nomads. Maybe you left before you were ready. Maybe the gigs you expected to get fell through. Maybe clients decided not to pay you. Maybe you got robbed or scammed and had to borrow money to get back home.

It's humiliating, frustrating, and very easy to feel stuck or helpless. To top it all off, everyone's treating you like a charity case. Yeah, this sucks. All the same, it's time to swallow your pride, admit what didn't work, and move on.

Everyone's situation is going to be different, but making some money needs to be your priority. It's time to take stock — what happened? Take a job, even if it's beneath you, and redouble your efforts to find the sort of work you want to take.

Adopting a new home

You've had an epic trip, and while you *could* continue the nomadic journey, you feel like settling down. Where? The world really is your oyster.

Obtaining residency, a long-term visa, and/or that country's passport are natural things to start researching. Be aware these will require a lot of time and energy to obtain if not in your home country, and goes outside the scope of this book. Some countries offer second passports as part of an economic program, requiring you to invest a five or six-figure amount of money in the country, and are often discussed by proponents of flag theory. Be sure to research whether you're expected to apply from your home country or inside the country in question, along with other specifics to the process. Be on the lookout for signs of stability — the last thing you want is to discover the program is being discontinued or stopped!

Networking and finding work

This one's a challenge for some. If you know you're back for good, you might be tempted to switch from whatever worked for you while you traveled to a more traditional job. Getting your resume / CV updated, along with the actual job search and finding work-appropriate clothes, will keep you busy!

How do I explain to employers what I've been doing the last few months / several years? For obvious reasons, this is going to be different for everyone. To your credit, though, you likely held any number of jobs, gigs, or positions, and helped any number of people accomplish any number things. Reach out to them and ask to use them as references, testimonials, or portfolio pieces where possible, and don't be afraid to tackle the time gap on your resume / CV. There's a certain corporate-speak that's deemed acceptable on a resume / CV, so try not to get too cute with it. Many traditional jobs these days use software to filter through resumes, and there's definitely a trick to using the 'right' or 'best' words to get through the machine filtering part.

When it comes to interviews, emphasizing your unique experiences is something best done by sharing your creative solutions, cultural insights, and personal examples. Focus on the results you delivered, and aim to mention *how* you did it in passing, if at all. Few will be impressed you held a conference call at 3am, but many will be impressed by the fact that you saved a client $10,000, or delivered a project ahead of schedule and under budget.

You may also need to demonstrate proficiency in the tools or programs used in today's workplaces. This will depend on what field you're in and the number of people you'll be working with, naturally. Budget some time to get caught up if you haven't been using those same tools in your digital nomad life. These tools might have been the ones you replaced with newer, more cutting-edge stuff, and can feel like a step backward. Remember that traditional jobs can't and don't run efficiently as you do, but they are still around.

If you're back for good…

As part of the 'settling into home' process, take stock of the products and services you currently use (and more importantly, pay for). Something like a mail receiving service won't be needed once you've decided to stay somewhere for a longer period of time. Once cancelled, go through your bank or credit card statements to ensure you're no longer being charged for any subscriptions you no longer need.

It's probably time to update your wardrobe as well — exactly what you'll want or need will depend on where you're working or the new climate, but it's safe to say a trip to the store is in order.

It's going to feel a bit exciting, just like any new place does at first, but it will also feel a little mundane at times. Remember why you've come here, find the routines that make you happy, and take full advantage of what the area has to offer. There's bound to be some great groups or places to join on a more permanent basis that would have been difficult to fully appreciate as a nomad.

Leaving again might feel harder… or infinitely easier

You can't leave us again! Not before sharing more stories… your family or some friends might say. Maybe they can join you, or perhaps they have a point. Make this visit a chance to connect, while you're there, and then actually follow through on those promises to stay connected as you travel.

Another element is the place or area itself. It can feel like a lot has changed, and you've barely scratched the surface on catching up. *You can't leave yet!* the city might say. If you're on a deadline, make the most of the time to see the sights and have those awesome catch-up moments with friends.

Some nomads will go back long enough to realize everything they hated about the city is only worse now — and they're counting down the days until they can leave again. Sometimes it's the people that make the place worth visiting, and sometimes it's not. Enjoy the company you choose, and try to embrace the things you might have missed as a nomad.

Wrapping it all up

Returning home can bring an overwhelming flood of emotions, no matter why you might be returning. Like so many other aspects of a digital nomad journey, it's going to be different for everyone. Take it easy on yourself through this process, just like you do when arriving at a new place.

What's next?

Wherever your next stop is, remember there are often multiple ways to arrive — planes, buses, trains, and boats may all be an option. At stake is more comfort, a lower price, an ability to take more stuff with you, and more convenience. While anything that involves crossing an ocean will likely mean a plane ticket (unless a cruise option is worth considering), any travels to neighboring or nearby countries ought to include the train and bus options where they exist.

Traveling philosophy

Some people traveling or being a traveler makes you wiser. More worldly. More refined. Or maybe just *better*, in ways that matter to yourself and others. Let's take this back a notch: **you are not a 'better person' simply because you've traveled to umpteen countries.** One does not evolve onto a higher plane of existence simply because your passport receives its umpteenth stamp.

Your traveling *does* allow you, however, to meet a greater portion of the world's cultures and mindsets, and hopefully appreciate them more deeply in the process. Even as you travel to more countries, it's still all too easy to revert to your bubble. This goes double if you're around other nomads or traveling companions that reinforce that 'bubble'. It's fine to have your apartment or room as a space to be comfortable in, but this space is not the reason you came to a new country.

To that end, I challenge you to C.A.R.E. while you travel:

- **Be curious** — go down the side streets, try the weird-looking food, ask questions, and research whatever interests you.
- **Be adaptable** — go with the flow, whether it's colder than expected, taking longer than expected, or just not what you expected.

- **Be respectful** — listen with respect, keep an open mind, dress appropriately, know local laws and customs, and so on.
- **Be an explorer** — take tours led by locals. Go beyond official government sources for information and look for community maps that highlight offbeat offerings. Seek out alternative tours and small businesses.

Some pro-tips that didn't fit anywhere else

After you've lived abroad for awhile, you'll have a few of these too.

- Learn the local term for 'tap water', and use it when requesting drinks at restaurants. Provided the local tap water is drinkable and you would otherwise be drinking bottled water, it's an easy way to save some money.
- Before arriving at an airport, take a look at the airport's website to see whether there's more stuff to see / do / eat **before** security or **after** security. Alternatively, the free apps GateGuru and FLIO are both good at offering plenty of info about the airport. Either way, it's no fun to be on the 'wrong' side of security when you're starving.
- Restaurants in Spain and some Spanish-speaking countries in South America offer a *menu del dia* (menu of the day) — typically a set-price three-course meal with a drink that's often one of the cheaper offerings. If we saw a restaurant had it, we'd usually just get that instead of bothering with the menu. (A *table d'hote* or *prix fixe* are similar, but those terms are primarily used in fancier restaurants.)
- Quite a few popular museums and tourist attractions have a free admission day once a month (and sometimes more frequently). Look it up, then add it to your calendar.
- While taking photos, take them in both portrait (vertical) and landscape (horizontal) orientation. You never know which version you'll like better. Take pictures of signs and

entrances to help link the place name to where you were (and perhaps more importantly, when you were there).
- If taking pictures on your phone, ensure locations are added to the metadata — GPS coordinates can be recorded to help you remember where something was. This is usually in Location Services on iOS or Geo Tags on Android.
- When asking locals where a place is, don't just listen to an address or vague directions you'll forget five seconds later. Pull out your phone, open Google Maps, then have them find it on the map. Zoom in as much as necessary, then tap and hold on that location to bring up the 'save' menu.
- Break larger currency notes at department stores, larger grocery stories, chain convenience stores, and chain restaurants. The larger the store or the better known it is, the better chance it can break a larger bill. I've been amazed at how little cash the world keeps on hand to make change.
- Ironing boards make for a perfect addition to a desk, from holding paperwork to keeping stuff organized.
- If you're a fan of going to the movies, know whether a country prefers to dub in a local language voice actors or subtitle their films. Most children's and animated films will be dubbed almost anywhere you go, but the practice of dubbing or subtitling varies by country. Look it up before spending money on a movie you can't understand!

Conclusions

I hate to leave you here. I really hope that you've learned about the digital nomad lifestyle, what it takes to make it work, and started down a path of your choosing. No more 'path of least resistance', no more 'doing as you're told', no more 'doing what you're supposed to do', and no more 'doing what society wants you to do'. Your life is yours to live, not your mom's, dad's, brother's, sister's, spouse's, partner's, or anyone else.

I also hope this book answered your questions, including many you hadn't thought to ask. At the same time, I really hope you'll join the communities of digital nomads that seem to be everywhere. From Internations to Facebook groups and from Couchsurfing meet-ups to people you meet as you travel, like-minded people are all around you. There's even a Facebook group specifically for readers of this book — facebook.com/groups/becomingadigitalnomad.

I'd also like to extend to you an invitation. Beyond this book, I consult with people one-on-one via Skype about the digital nomad lifestyle. These one-hour sessions are tailor-made to clarify your goals, manage your expectations, answer your questions, connect you to resources, and discuss your specific concerns. Whichever step you're on in this digital nomad journey, a one-hour consultation can save you countless hours of potential mis-steps and uncertainty. See becomingadigitalnomad.com/consulting for information on scheduling an appointment.

Finally, I'd love to hear from you. Did I miss something? Do you have feedback? Want to share your story? Have a suggestion for the next edition of this book? See becomingadigitalnomad.com/contact or e-mail chrisbacke@gmail.com.

Please also consider sharing your review with the world on Amazon. Thanks so much for reading!

Made in the USA
Middletown, DE
07 July 2020